I've known Daun Whittaker for many years, and if there's one thing you can say about Daun is that she has a heart for people. She not only wants individuals to prosper but longs to see them healed, delivered, restored, and set free.

She truly believes that love is the greatest gift, and that is our connection with people and with our heavenly Father. She strongly feels that love is the motivating factor in ministry.

Her life's expression is one of giving and one of charity. She exemplifies virtually every day the Bible verse that exhorts us to prefer others over ourselves.

In this book, she motivates us to love as the Father loves. The Bible says there is no greater love than this, that one lays down their life for another. Daun lives that most every day as she pours herself out as a drink offering that others may experience the love of the Father.

I've personally been involved in healing ministry for approximately 40 years, with 20 years in the Healing Rooms ministry out of Spokane, Washington. And I often teach that love is the only motivation for ministry. If we have not love, as the Bible teaches, we're nothing more than a clanging gong and a sounding symbol. Many people wonder why their prayers are not answered, even though they seem to have great faith. The answer is simple—Galatians 5:6 says that faith works by love.

As a northeast regional director for the Healing Room ministry, I wholeheartedly endorse this work. If you let it, it will transform your life and transform you more into the image of God, who is love.

Dr. Rev. Vincent Aquilino
International Association of Healing Rooms (IAHR)
Regional Director for New York and New England

CHANGE YOUR MIND

AND

CHANGE YOUR LIFE

Your Guide to
Emotional Health and Fulfillment

DAUN WHITTAKER

Published by HigherLife Development Services Inc.
PO Box 623307, Oviedo, Florida 32762
www.ahigherlife.com

ISBN: 978-1-958211-60-1 (Paperback)
ISBN: 978-1-958211-59-5 (ebook)

Library of Congress Control Number: 1-12759598721

Printed in the United States of America.
10 9 8 7 6 5 4 3 2 1

DEDICATION

I am grateful to all the many people that have contributed time and encouragement to the writing of this book. Even though circumstances made it take much longer than it should, I have been greatly blessed by everybody that took the time to make sure this book was written.

First, I would like to acknowledge my very supportive husband, Bill Whittaker, who when proofreading, often discovered that he was a subject of a story with an assumed name!

Special thanks to Laura Bishop who went through the book and offered stellar advice as well as proofreading. Thank you, Ellen King, for not only being a great editor, but also patient when I needed extra time, and someone I can now call my friend.

Thank you, Angela Livingston, for making sure I had uninterrupted writing time and providing for me so I could write.

Most of all, I thank my heavenly Father for giving me the privilege to be part of so many lives and the experiences which made all of this possible for His glory!

CONTENTS

INTRODUCTION

Since 2009, I have been a counselor in private practice; before that, I was the executive director of a mental health organization, and have been involved in nonprofit development and administration for most of my adult life. I began walking with the Lord in 2008. With my new hunger for the Word came the clear understanding that mental health and counseling practices made more sense from a scriptural perspective. I recognized that I used many principles in my counseling that had biblical roots.

I founded a ministry called Victory Transformation that helps people who are homeless, addicted, and disenfranchised. It is my overwhelming experience that faith in Christ through discipleship truly is the answer. I have watched people transform before my eyes, and recognize that I am privileged to be part of their journey.

The principles that follow are a collection of strategies and tools that have been effective in my counseling practice and personal experiences. My purpose is to share these experiences and observations so that you may gain new perspective, develop strategies, and understand the underlying issues and concerns that reduce our joy and peace day-to-day. My intention was to create a document that anyone could read and use. However, it's important that you understand that these observations and experiences are not the *only* way, and may not even represent the *best* way for you.

Jesus worked hard not to offend people, but sometimes the truth is offensive; in 1 Peter 2:8 Jesus was referred to as a "rock of offense" which meant that some people would stumble in trying to understand his message. As you read through this, if you find some of the concepts offensive, remember that they are a perspective of truth that you may find helpful if you take the time to consider them. I know that if I'd had this guidance in my early days, it would have been very helpful in working and raising a family.

I strongly believe in the power of EEE: Encouragement, Edification, and Exhortation. Since I lean towards solutions-focused therapy and believe in the power of building on successes, I pray for wisdom and guidance frequently. It is vital to meet people where they are, and speak truth into their lives with a right heart.

When we commune with one another and God in prayer, mountains move.

Prayer should always be our first line of defense, not a last resort. When we commune with one another and God in prayer, mountains move. Even medical professionals at cancer centers and hospitals who profess to being atheist or agnostic encourage prayer because they have seen consistent, positive results because of it. In my own life, prayer has been responsible for so many good things!

Love *is* the greatest gift. Connection between people and our heavenly Father makes all the difference. Through Christ,

I love the people that God has brought to me. This book is a culmination of my experience in being led and used by God to help people heal and enjoy a better quality of life.

Besides the work that I am so passionate about, I love my family and friends. I am married to the love of my life, Bill Whittaker, and we have five adult children and one grandson. I am truly blessed to be able to share my experiences, so that others may live blessed lives for God's glory!

Daun M. Whittaker

PRINCIPLE 1:
BE INTENTIONAL!

Wise people think before they act;
fools don't—and even brag
about their foolishness.
(Proverbs 13:16)

One of the most important principles to live by is to know the outcome you want to achieve before you speak or behave. An outcome is the consequence produced by a plan, so it is largely the result of the choices we make. Achieving this requires intentionality on our part.

I've written a lot of grant proposals. They require the creation of a plan with intent of producing particular outcomes for which I am seeking funding. On a personal level, every decision we make results in some outcome, even if unintended. That means you have a choice if you want to create positive outcomes. So *be intentional*. Be thoughtful before you speak or act. Matthew 12:36 (NIV) tells us "that everyone will have to give account on the day of judgment for every empty word they have spoken." Some versions replace the word *empty* with *careless* or *idle*. It is evident that intentionality is important in our interactions with people. Being intentional will help produce favorable outcomes.

This doesn't mean that if you are intentional, *every outcome* will be favorable. Sometimes our poor choices not only produce unfavorable results, but can even offer a plethora of them. For instance, if you got a speeding ticket, you may have to choose between paying an attorney to represent you, so you do not get points on your license, or meeting with the judge to try and negotiate the ticket first. Neither option is favorable; both cost time and money. You could also make a third choice: just forget about the whole thing like it never happened. In Rush's song "Freewill," Geddy Lee sings, "If you choose not to decide, you still have made a choice."[1] That is so true.

Sometimes our anxiety over a situation causes us to try to avoid everything about it. Avoidance and procrastination often lead to unfavorable outcomes and heighten our growing sense of powerlessness. Without intentionality, your circumstances or feelings control your decision-making, rendering you powerless, just as you feared you would be. So when you do not intentionally consider an outcome, you still create one.

Oftentimes these outcomes are the worst of all. If the person in our ticket scenario just ignored court and dismissed the appearance of the ticket, it's likely that they would get hefty fines and maybe even lose their license. You might think, *How ridiculous. Why would anyone not take care of something like that?* It happens all the time in a variety of areas.

---

1   Peart, "Freewill" (Le Studio, Morin Heights, QC, Canada, n.d.).

Avoidance is a primary coping strategy when a situation causes anxiety. This does not excuse inaction, but it does explain it. Sometimes our avoidance may be subtle. For example, Joan made a nasty comment to Don about his unprofessionalism in the form of a joke. Don is hurt, but does not want to create strife so he keeps quiet and politely laughs. In time, this offense grows into resentment and slowly erodes their friendship. Don avoids talking to Joan and even begins talking about her with his colleagues, slipping in negative remarks about her when he can. Her comment + his avoidance = loss of friendship. By now, Joan senses something is wrong and asks Don about it, but his resentment has built a wall of unforgiveness inside, so he flatly says, "Nothing is wrong. I am fine. Thanks for asking." It's easy to see how avoiding the speeding ticket could escalate into a bad situation, but in a subtler situation in which a friend says something offensive, it may not be so apparent.

When you do not intentionally direct yourself toward a specific outcome, your emotions may dictate that outcome. Your feelings are in the driver's seat. Emotions are powerful. Emotions indicate what you believe during a short period of time, but they are not *what* you believe. They only indicate a temporary state; they do not indicate what we believe, wish to accomplish, or our primary purpose.

My dear friend, Helena Davis, used the example of the lights on a car's dashboard. If the engine light comes on it tells you there is a problem with the engine. The light is not *the problem* with the engine. If you reset the computer on the car and the engine indicator light goes out, you did not repair the problem with the engine. That problem is still there in need of attention. Making decisions solely based on your feelings about a situation may result in a seemingly desired outcome, but may still produce undesirable or unintended consequences. You may deeply wound someone or create offense that may harm relationship among other things. If we are operating strictly by the indicators, we may not achieve the outcomes we are trying to achieve, and if we do, we might create new difficulties in the process. This is so unnecessary.

Here are a couple of helpful examples that look at everyday situations and illustrate the power of intentionally asking yourself: "What outcome do I wish to achieve?"

Christine is the parent of a seventeen–year-old daughter, Kayla. Christine works hard to be healthy. There is a history of heart disease on her side of the family, and a history of obesity and heart disease on Matt, her husband's side too. Christine is extremely concerned about Kayla's weight, so she tries to engage Kayla in a conversation about it.

She lets Kayla know that sitting around and binge watching episodes of *Vampire Diaries* on Netflix is not good for her. She accuses Kayla of being overweight. Kayla becomes defensive and feels hurt, and begins texting her boyfriend for support. She is crying and wounded. Christine, sensing she is not getting through to her, becomes even more emphatic. Kayla storms off to her room, crying. Christine is flustered. What could have changed the result of this conversation?

Christine needed to consider the outcome she wanted to achieve prior to that conversation. Since she did not, her emotions (the indicators of her beliefs) controlled the conversation. She is actually concerned for her daughter's health and well-being and loves her very much, but that's not what came across to her daughter. Fear drove the conversation.

Imagine allowing the turn signals in our cars to dictate our direction. This sounds silly, but this is exactly what we are doing when we let our feelings or impulses choose our direction for us. Turn signals only indicate the direction (outcome) *we already consciously chose.* They are only indicators to the people around us.

If Christine would have thought about the outcome, she might have said to herself, *I am worried about Kayla's weight and her health, especially with our family history. I want to help her understand the significance of this problem, so she can be healthy. I want Kayla to be healthy.* Once Christine thought about her outcome, it would have naturally changed her approach to Kayla. It would have been clear that coming at this sensitive problem the way she did would be hurtful and offensive. Being focused on what she was trying to achieve would have resulted in a more effective (and more pleasant) conversation.

Joe gets home from work at 5:00. Emily, his wife, is preparing dinner. Derek, the couple's four-year-old son, is excited to see his daddy. Joe likes to sit down and watch the local news when he gets home, especially the sports and weather forecast. He sits on the couch, switches on the news, and puts up his feet. Derek is playing with airplanes in front of the TV, running around the living room, arms extended with his planes, making engine noises and laughing. The sports highlights begin, while Derek is screeching as he lands one of his planes. Joe erupts, yelling at Derek to sit down.

"Can't you see I am trying to watch this?" he screams. Crushed, the little boy cries, still standing in front of the television. Joe cannot see or hear it. Instead, his son is crying loudly, his wife is now also upset, and Joe is angry.

If he would have considered the outcome he was trying to achieve, this situation could have turned out differently. He might have thought about Derek being excited and playing loudly while he was trying to watch the sports highlights. He could have said, "Derek, come sit with Daddy and play quietly on the couch for a bit. When the news is over, I will play airplanes with you." Derek would have been filled with anticipation at the thought of this time with his dad, and been directed into another activity. This would have resulted in the outcome Joe was trying to achieve. It certainly would have resulted in a better outcome than the one he got.

It is important to be honest about the outcome you are trying to achieve. Once, I was arguing with my husband (this has definitely happened more than once!), and I was armed with an angry remark that I knew would hit the mark. I suddenly realized my outcome *was* to hurt him because he had hurt me. Once I saw this, I backed down from the argument. I quickly confessed that I was offended by what he said and was seeking to repay his hurt with hurt. Proverbs 28:13 states that "whoever conceals their sins does not prosper, but the one who confesses and renounces them finds mercy."

We both apologized and enjoyed the rest of our evening. That would not have happened had I not asked myself about the outcome I was trying to achieve. We might have spent the rest of our evening in separate rooms instead.

Asking yourself about the outcome you want to achieve takes some practice. It is easy to see what could have been in hindsight, but we must be proactive about it. When we take the time to recognize the need to do this in advance, our lives can be significantly different. Choices should lead, feelings should follow. Allowing our feelings to have the lead can bring about hurt, offenses, and impulsive decision-making. If we take a moment and consider what is going on and what we want, we are much more likely to live at peace with others and make sensible, life-changing choices.[2]

When I am counseling, this principle is often discussed in the second session. I say this rhythmically so it is easy to remember. (Emphasize the words in all caps):

WHAT is the OUTCOME I WANT to ACHIEVE?

This is so simple and yet it is so easily dismissed. Only when we intentionally and consciously put this into practice do we see better results. Because we are focused on them, our desired outcomes are more effectively obtained.

Seeking outcomes is a necessary first step to ordering our priorities. If we don't have clear, intentional outcomes, it is hard to prioritize effectively. Therefore, we find ourselves in a rut, feeling like we have no control. The outcome of the next principle will add some definition and perspective to this, so that we may prioritize effectively.

---

2   Cynthia E. Cryder, Stephen Springer, and Carey K. Morewedge, "Guilty Feelings, Targeted Actions," *Personality and Social Psychology Bulletin* 38, no. 5 (2012): pp. 607–618, https://doi.org/10.1177/0146167211435796.

PRINCIPLE 2:
TIME VERSUS PRIORITY

Wherever your treasure is,
there the desires of your heart will
also be. (Luke 12:34)

We live busy, hectic lifestyles. As a child, I remember waiting impatiently for the popcorn in the kettle on the stove to pop, so we could add butter and go in the living room and watch a movie. Today, I impatiently wait in the kitchen for three minutes for the microwave to do the same thing in much less time, and I'm still impatient. As things are getting faster and more efficient, we are viewing time differently.

Often when I am counseling, I discover that the same people who don't have time to have lunch with a friend so they can mend a relationship will spend twice that time on social media. The same people who do not have time to call their parents or visit the hospital spend a significant amount of time browsing the Internet, watching TV, or playing games on their phone.

I have counseled a number of people who were required to call a doctor, family member, or some other significant contact as "homework" for counseling. Routinely, when I asked if the individual had made the phone call, they say, "I didn't have the time."

I explore this with them, asking, "Are you sure?" We always come to the conclusion that they did have time. They could have done it. What does this mean? It means the task was not a priority.

This is a significant differentiation. We must say, *It is not a priority to me* instead of believing we do not have time. We must see it for what it is. The fact is that it *is* okay if some things are not priorities—even if others think they should be priorities. But all of us must decide what our priorities are.

Barry has a young family and is a full-time contractor. When someone at church asked him to build a deck, Barry politely declined because he would have had to use the time he spends with his daughters to get it done. Barry has strong boundaries regarding his family time.

Your boundaries are your own, set by you. Even though they can potentially inconvenience people, you have every right to establish healthy boundaries. In this example, it is easy to understand why this young father and husband said no to the request. However, it's important to understand that his decision was based, not just on the time he would have to expend, but on its value. The extra side job just was not as important as everything else competing for his time.

Your boundaries are your own, set by you.

We must discern our priorities and what we can accomplish in the time we have. Why? The answer is twofold. When we say we don't have time that does not mean we are responsible for what we don't have time to accomplish. When you don't have time, it implies you are so busy that you couldn't help but to not make that phone call or complete that task. I rarely run into people who are truly that busy and I am surrounded by busy, successful people.

When John and Melissa came for marriage counseling, John often stated that he felt he wasn't important to Melissa anymore, and that her friends were more important than he was. He traveled quite a bit for his job, and was often hurt that she did not call him routinely or make herself available when he called. She shared that she was too busy with her job and everything she had going on every day to tend to that too. She insisted that she did not have time to talk to John as often as he wanted. We did a time study and took a good look at Melissa's schedule. She worked six hours a day at a local hotel doing housekeeping. Melissa's Screen Time app showed that she was spending over three hours a day on social media and additional time playing games on her phone.

The Screen Time analysis was not used to blame or point fingers; it was used to expose the truth that John was not a priority. His feelings of being unimportant to his wife were validated, but this wasn't the end of their story. It was the beginning. Once Melissa was walking in the truth, she was able to share that she felt inadequate in their marriage, and had for a long time. She also struggled with John's constant condescending and sarcastic remarks. As a result, she was spending more time with her girlfriends who were supportive and encouraging.

Once we were able to reframe "I don't have time" into "it is not a priority," we were able to identify and work on the real problems more efficiently. Melissa began sharing her feelings and felt safe to share. (Prior to this, she had insisted she simply did not have time to talk to John as he desires, and followed this with her laundry list of all the things she had to do to justify that. This had prevented her from being responsible for her actions or validating and recognizing her own feelings and concerns in the marriage. Her insistence that she did not have time allowed her to avoid significant issues in her marriage. Now both her *and her husband's* issues were on the table and could be addressed.

In a culture in which we excuse things so easily, it is important that we speak, understand, and own our personal responsibility.

In a culture in which we excuse things so easily, it is important that we speak, understand, and own our personal responsibility. When we don't consider our own role in choosing our priorities, it is easy to believe that either we don't have time or that it has gotten away from us somehow. Once we view the world through this lens, we no longer have personal responsibility or control over the situation. On the other hand, when we admit that we didn't call the doctor today because we had not made it a priority, it not only changes the lens, but also compels us to examine our priorities and how we made that determination.

This was the case with Mindy. Mindy said she wanted to go to school, but she struggled with following through with her plans, and frequently avoided doing the next thing due to her anxiety about her self-worth. We discussed her interest in school, and I challenged her. I gave her an assignment to meet with the enrollment team at Cayuga Community College. This was an information-gathering assignment at the school she wished to attend. This meeting needed to take place before we met again.

During our next session, I could tell Mindy was anxious. When I asked her how she was doing, she quickly replied that she had not had time to do the assignment. After some encouragement, I asked her to share how she had spent her week, so we could identify what had prevented her from going to the college. As she spoke, she quickly recognized that there was no evidence to support the idea that she lacked the time. In fact, the reverse was true and she was embarrassed by how much time she *did* have to complete the task!

So we reframed it as an issue of prioritizing. She shared that it wasn't a priority because she was afraid to move forward with the goal. When she looked at that based on priority instead of time, she was able to clearly see how her feelings about herself were hindering her movement. Sometimes when we understand how our beliefs impact our choices, we can grow and heal. If Mindy had continued to believe that she didn't have time, she would have continued operating in avoidance with no prospects for future growth.

Mindy and I scheduled her next session at the college admission's office. She started school last fall and averaged a 3.5 GPA her first semester. She had taken a step and her excellent progress is going a long way to helping her see herself differently.

It is important to understand that change happened when Mindy saw the truth in her situation. I just presented information to her in a different way than she had been perceiving it before. Sometimes people are not ready (or able) to take responsibility, make changes, or see things from a different perspective, so this is often a delicate process. I know it reads like Mindy came in, presented her situation, we worked to get her in college, and within a short time, she was there and succeeding as a student. This was not the case. She spent three months identifying the beliefs she carried in her heart about who she was and what she could do. Her wrong beliefs about her self-worth and strong feelings of inadequacy made it difficult for her to see the possibilities for her future.

When someone cannot imagine positive outcomes and prioritize, the fruit they produce reflects that. After all, we know people by their fruit.

PRINCIPLE 3:
YOU KNOW THEM
BY THEIR FRUIT

> You can identify them by their
> fruit, that is, by the way they
> act. Can you pick grapes from
> thornbushes, or figs from thistles?
> (Matthew 7:16)

Society always seeks to understand. It is part of the human condition to assign meaning to everything. Sometimes we don't do this correctly. For instance, I have had numerous sinus infections in my life. In spite of this, when I experience the first symptom of extreme tiredness, I consistently attribute it to being overworked instead of recognizing what it really is. The next day, my glands swell up and I have sinus pain. Every time this happens, I admonish myself to no avail for not recognizing that it was my usual problem. We need to assign meaning to things to understand and navigate our world. We are designed to do this.

A fruit tree may look beautiful, but its purpose is to bear fruit, so we judge it by what it produces, not how it looks overall. As referenced above, Jesus told us that we will "know them by their fruit." In that passage, He is referring to the words and deeds of false prophets, but He uses this principle elsewhere too. In John 13:34–35 (NIV), He commands His disciples thus: "Love one another. As I have loved you, so you must love one another." He further explains that by this love, others will know "you are my disciples." Jesus provided concrete examples of what love looks like and the fruit that it bears.

This may seem to be a strange topic for a book about observations and experiences in my Christian counseling but it has many applications. Our culture is teaching us to judge motive, and reason everything out. This not only is impractical; it is often misleading and unbiblical. I created a chart to help illustrate: Please note that *judgment* is *not* synonymous with *condemnation*. We are not called to condemn people, but should do everything in love with a right heart. According to *Webster's Unabridged Dictionary*, *judgment* is "an operation of the mind involving comparison and discrimination (discernment)" to form an opinion or evaluation.[3] What follows is a simple illustration only meant to foster understanding of the principle, not explore every facet of it.

A. How it should be:
     Fruit produced —> Judgment —> Conclusion

     In other words, first look at the fruit that was produced (the actions, words, and behaviors). Judge the fruit and then come to a conclusion. Here's an example: A man

3   "Judgment Definition & Meaning," *Webster's Unabridged Dictionary*, part of the public domain at Project Gutenberg.

walked into the Victory Center because he was homeless. His wife had kicked him out of the house due to his increasing abuse of oxycodone. The fruit produced by his drug addiction was homelessness and the destruction of his marriage. If he tells me he has everything under control and doesn't need treatment or help, the fruit is telling me something very different. I cannot force him to get treatment, but when I judge the fruit, my conclusion will be that he needs a place to stay, help with his opioid addiction, and help to reconcile his marriage. It is a simple, straightforward equation, which leads me to have great compassion for both the man and his wife.

B. How it is often done instead:
    Fruit produced —> Motive behind fruit —>
    Judgment —> Justification —> Conclusion

This equation may lead to an outcome that is devoid of personal responsibility, and therefore untenable and likely to foster a sense of entitlement. If I were to plug the above scenario into this equation, it may look like this: A man walks into the Victory Center because he is homeless. His wife kicked him out of the house due to his increasing abuse of oxycodone. He is homeless and losing his marriage as a result of his drug abuse. If he tells me he has everything under control and doesn't need treatment or help, the fruit produced is still telling me something very different. However, in accordance with the above illustration, now I am going to look at the motives behind the fruit. He may share that his wife is a controlling person who is very demanding. Five years ago, he had been prescribed with oxycodone for a leg injury, but for the most part, he takes it to deal with his wife's verbal abuse and controlling behavior. *He* doesn't need help; *she* needs to change. If she would change, he would no longer need to take the pills.

Now my judgment is based on the fruit and the motivation (or reasoning) behind it. This may cloud my judgment. I may believe that his wife is verbally abusive and he is just trying to cope. I may overlook or justify the other factors (fruit)—he is unemployed, justifying it because the stress at home was so great that it affected his ability to go to work and so, he was fired. I may conclude that his marriage is irreconcilable if she does not get help with her abusive behavior. Instead of compassion, I feel pity. I may also foster his sense of entitlement and unwittingly contribute to his continued drug abuse. Let's look at another example.

I run an outreach mission that serves the homeless. Many people coming into our shelter were newly released from prison. One such individual was Jonah. A staff member was meeting with Jonah, and going over the rules of the Victory House where he would be staying. Jonah, with arms crossed and "know-it-all" expression kept repeating, "I know, I know" after nearly every rule. He also claimed that he didn't need help to find a job and knew what he needed to do. We were trying to help Jonah achieve lasting success and lead a good life independent of public support, so we needed to be able to assess his needs and his plan for the future (the outcome).

If we employed **Model A**, we would look at the fruit produced and assess it based on Jonah's words, posturing, behavior, and attitude. These attested to Jonah being prideful and uninterested in our help. The judgment we might make is that in humility he would be teachable and gain confidence and understanding. The volunteer advocates would then pray, counsel, and love him daily. We would all model humility and gratitude, and he would eventually see the fruit of this in others, and understand that when he humbled himself and demonstrated gratitude, we could help him. Until then, our helping resources would go to people whose fruit demonstrated the desire and willingness to take real steps toward positive growth and change.

Now let's look at **Model B** relative to Jonah and his fruit. The assessment in **B** looks at the motivation or reasoning behind the fruit produced. This may result in justification which could look like this instead: Jonah just got out of prison and his pride is a product of being in prison. This justification may be an assumption. As our reasoning leads to justification, it may also lead to excusing him: "Oh, no wonder he is acting like he has a chip on his shoulder. He has been through so much." The conclusion we come to in **B** may be something like this: *We need to help him feel love and trust. We need to show him that he can have a good life. Once that happens, then he will be able to receive what we have to offer.* Sometimes we get into trouble when we use this understanding and its resulting justification to excuse the behavior. We might even take this course of action, further excusing and enabling him: *Jonah made some real derogatory remarks to John at the house last night. I know that violates our rules and discipline is needed, but he has been through so much and this will pass once we help him to reintegrate.* This does not help Jonah achieve and sustain the quality of life he needs and is seeking.

Model **B** becomes about what *we* need to do to help Jonah. It puts the responsibility of his success on *us.* Note that Model **A** states that the volunteers will pray, counsel, and love him daily. In Model **B**, once we reason and justify, it becomes about what the advocates and volunteers can do for him, *not what he can do.* This model requires little personal responsibility so there is little, if any, growth.

> Small successes in behavioral changes, attitudes, and coping can empower a person and give a healthy foundation on which to build.

It's true that motives are important, but assessing the fruit people produce offers them the opportunity to be proactive and effective at facilitating growth and change. Small successes in behavioral changes, attitudes, and coping can empower a person and give a healthy foundation on which to build.

As a program dedicated to serving people like Jonah, we need to understand that the only way to help them *feel* love and trust is to model love and trust in relationships. Forgiving and not condemning. Helping someone *feel* love and trust is not the same as helping someone to love and trust. Feelings are never wrong, but sometimes the beliefs they are based on are. As a result, we may be encouraging entitlement or encouraging hurtful or negative behavior. All *do* need to do is love him with a right heart. As Christians, we should be walking in the fullness of the fruit of the Spirit—the result of the work of the Holy Spirit in our lives. The fruit of the Spirit, found in Galatians 5:22–23, is made up of the following nine qualities: love, joy, peace, patience, kindness, goodness, faithfulness, gentleness, and self-control. It is important that we know others by their fruit.

As previously stated, our loving someone is not part of the outcome in either equation. It is how we are supposed to treat each other. Period. All the time. This happens independent of goal setting or working with an individual. We walk in love. People see it. We cannot help someone *feel* loved. We can just love them. You know us by our fruit.

We demonstrate love by being a good friend, being compassionate and kind, and by walking in truth—listening and affirming. In John 15:12 (NLT), Jesus says, "This is my commandment: Love each other in the same way I have loved you." As His disciples, we seek to love each other as Christ loves us.

How can you help someone feel trust? By demonstrating honor, integrity, and truth in our words and deeds. We must communicate well. These are actions that we walk out. We may not be able to help someone *feel* trust, but we can *be* trustworthy. They will know us by our fruit.

Additionally, when we use reasoning (remember, we assign meaning to everything), we sometimes find that our reasoning is incorrect. For instance, upon further examination, we found Jonah's prideful behavior was a factor in putting Jonah in prison in the first place.

So, what's the answer? Love him, disciple and counsel him, and provide tools to help him learn to change. But we cannot take responsibility for his change; he must do that. We worked with Jonah on the premise that we "know them by their fruit." After a week, Jonah began to soften and often sought out conversation with the volunteer advocates. He began to smile and slowly opened himself to correction. It was in humility that he found a job in construction as a laborer. My friend would have never hired him had he walked on the job site with the same attitude he had presented to our advocates in the beginning. Jonah is doing quite well now and periodically drops in to check on us. He is off parole, has his license, bought a truck, and is in a healthy relationship. He left our program about two and a half years ago.

This situation with Jonah turned out well, but it might not have. He could have continued with that chip on his shoulder, and may not have made the necessary changes as a result. He would have continued as he was—without a job and unlikely to grow personally on top of that. Eventually, he would probably have violated the rules at Victory House, violated parole, and landed back in prison. We have seen this scenario play out over and over again. Some blame these kinds of results on a broken system, but personal responsibility starts with the word *personal*.

What would not help Jonah? Assigning meaning to his situation based on reasoning. Excusing and justifying his behavior.

I have worked with many kids with behavioral challenges. One was eleven-year-old Austin who was diagnosed with

Autism Spectrum Disorder. He was high-functioning and quite intelligent. His mother told me that while shopping, Austin had wanted ice cream, and she had to say no because of their limited resources. What began as begging quickly escalated into a full-blown tantrum—jumping up and down and yelling. Sheila, his mother, got a quart of ice cream for him, thinking that she had not given in to him since she had not bought the half gallon he wanted.

"Why did you get him any ice cream at all if you couldn't afford it?" I asked. She immediately went into a long explanation justifying her decision because of his sensory issues and how difficult it was for him to regulate his emotions. I asked her who was going to justify his behavior when he was an adult and living on his own. Sheila paused, suddenly realizing that if Austin was ever going to live independently, he had to get this behavior under control. If we focus on the fruit and make a judgment, we are much more likely to choose to modify behavior instead of justifying it. I have a very high-functioning, adult son on the spectrum, and I worked very hard to understand the motives for his behavior, often justifying it at school with ready explanations for why he behaved the way he did. I was not wrong in my understanding; in fact, I was spot-on. Unfortunately, my accurate understanding did not serve my son well when he became an adult living independently, and later contributed to many difficulties he has had to overcome. My justifications hadn't done him any favors.

Here is another example. I counseled a teenage girl, Amber, who was very disrespectful to her parents. Her mother, Sharon, supported her in her behavior toward her father because he was also disrespectful and she didn't feel that he deserved it. Since Amber's disrespectful behavior was being justified by her father's—and Sharon excused it, Amber extended her behavior toward her teachers too. Sharon began getting calls at work and had multiple meetings with the principal. Much healing was needed in this family, but the fact that Amber was mimicking the bad behavior modeled by her dad did not excuse it or remove the consequences she had to face because of her own choices.

There is one last thing I want to touch on. Some of you may be reading this and feel that my approach is hard and lacking in compassion. Nothing could be further from the truth. In counseling, if minds change, behavior will follow. This is true in the reverse too. If behavior changes, the mind will follow. There really is truth in the old adage: Fake it until you make it, or as my good

If minds change, behavior will follow.

friend says: *Face* it until you make it. Have you ever been sad or upset about something, but knew you had to teach a class, wait on tables, or take your kids to the park in spite of how you felt? You had to behave like you were not upset so you did not adversely affect the well-being of the people you were serving. What happens? In most cases, our changed behavior changes our mindset, and our mood changes as well. This doesn't remove the reason we were upset, but we find that when we *choose* to change our behavior, our mind comes into alignment.

Our choices and actions culminate into fruit that people can see. We are called to make a judgment on this fruit. When we try and judge motives and feelings, we may be pacifying and find ourselves justifying bad behavior. Negative emotions serve a purpose too; they just don't feel good. Negative emotions—like guilt and sorrow—indicate when we need to apologize or change an action. Let's look at godly sorrow.

PRINCIPLE 4:
GODLY SORROW LEADS TO REPENTANCE

> For the kind of sorrow God wants
> us to experience leads us away
> from sin and results in salvation.
> There's no regret for that kind
> of sorrow. But worldly sorrow,
> which lacks repentance, results in
> spiritual death.
> (2 Corinthians 7:10)

I love this verse and use it often in counseling. Its application is broad but provides a helpful measure for people who are struggling with guilt. Let's look at it more closely. Paul's first letter to the Corinthians was very admonishing due to rampant immorality in the Corinthian church. The Corinthians were saved but were walking in sin. They were grieved over Paul's first letter which led to Paul's statement about godly sorrow in his second letter. Simply put, godly sorrow brings repentance that leads to salvation. Paul was not excusing the Corinthians' grief over their sinful behavior. It's important to note this. We live in a society whose mantra is seeking pleasure and avoiding pain above all else, at all costs. The fact is that there is a purpose for guilt and grief. We *should* lament over bad behavior. The godly sorrow Paul is referring to leads to true repentance, a turning away. It leads to change, growth, and resiliency. This builds character.

We have become accustomed to understanding bad behavior as opposed to correcting it. This leads us to often excusing it, even if it hurts someone. Feeling guilty about hurting someone is painful. Understandably, we want to escape and avoid feeling this way. However, experiencing repentance for the behavior that causes us this pain helps build character. In psychology, we would say that this grief (or guilt) promotes *reparative behavior*. The idea that feeling guilty is always bad leads us into entitlement. We are created in God's image. Science considers guilt a self-conscious negative emotion, and godly sorrow or guilt helps us correct bad behavior. Self-conscious negative emotions help us frame another's response to our words and behaviors. This helps protect relationships.

I counseled a couple early on in my counseling career named Sam and Judy. They had been married for twenty-six years and had three children between the ages of seven and twelve. One of Sam's good friends, Derek, was staying with the family for a time too. One day Sam came home for lunch and walked in on his wife having sex with Derek. This was both traumatic and painful. By the time they came for counseling, Sam was full of rage, and both of them were struggling with forgiveness.

Throughout counseling, Judy stated that she had been struggling for quite a while with feeling numb and lacking motivation. She shared with Sam how much she had wanted to *feel* again, which led to the act. She didn't know what was wrong with her.

It did turn out that Judy was on medication for depression and the dose and type of medication was responsible for these symptoms. We addressed the medication issues, but it was understood that the medication did not justify her behavior. Judy truly regretted what she had done. She sought forgiveness and changed the behavior, but the healing process was long and difficult. In time, repentance led to positive change in the marriage from both Judy and Sam. For instance, the couple changed aspects of their communication and intimacy. Judy got off the medication, bringing significant change. She became more communicative and engaged with her husband and family.

I am happy to say that this couple is going strong and has kept in touch with me over the years. In this case, it is easy to see that godly sorrow brought true repentance that led to salvation, leaving no regret. The Holy Spirit convicted Judy of her wrongdoing and this led to positive growth in her marriage and family.

Now let's look at the last part of that verse.

Worldly sorrow leads to death. What is worldly sorrow or worldly grief? Worldly sorrow is unrepentant and selfish regret. Picture a child who is being told to put down his tablet at the dinner table. Mom gives explicit instruction and much latitude to the child. He still does not obey. Finally, his mom gets frustrated and takes the tablet. She lets him know he cannot have it back until the next day. The child is now very apologetic, but this is not godly sorrow. This is worldly sorrow. Worldly sorrow is guilt without repentance.

Responses to worldly guilt are often shallow, selfish, and prideful. The child in the example feels guilty, but he doesn't want to change his behavior and put the tablet down. This is a learning process with children; but as adults, allowing this pattern of behavior leads to spiritual death, just as Paul wrote. If you live a lifestyle filled with apologies given when you are caught doing something wrong or when a negative consequence occurs, you are not growing and changing. You're just feeling bad in the moment and returning to your old ways again. No remorse. No difference. Just back in the same old rut where you started.

Here is another example. Aileen was a twenty-four-year old woman who was dating Jonathan, age twenty-three. Both lived in Syracuse. One night Jonathan had made plans with Aileen to go out to dinner and a show for their six-month anniversary. Justin, one of Jonathan's friends, got tickets to an SU game and all the guys were going to the game, and then going out afterwards. One of the guys had been promoted and was moving to North Carolina. Jonathan really wanted to go with his friends and spend time with Nate before he left for North Carolina, but he already had plans and knew that Aileen would be disappointed if he did not go to their celebration. On top of that, the tickets they had for the show were almost 300 dollars and nonrefundable.

How did Jonathan handle this? He lied. He told Aileen he was very sorry but he could not get out of work. Aileen was very disappointed, but because she was good-natured and understanding, she found another friend to go to dinner and the show with her.

Jonathan had a great time with his friends. Even though he felt guilty, he was glad he had made the decision he made. Every time the guilt came to the forefront of his mind, he justified it by thinking, *It was really important that I was there for Nate*, or *I spend all my time with Aileen; my friends need me too.* Note that his justifications were about him: not Nate, Aileen, or his friends. He did not intend to repent unless he got caught. To help ease his guilt, he made a vow to himself that he would never do that to Aileen again. After all, he really cared for her. The problem with guilt is that it can linger for a long time with someone until there is resolution, while true repentance provides resolution. Imagine having a guilt bank in your brain. Are you a collector or a processor?

Both worldly sorrow and false guilt have a negative impact on our bodies too.

False Guilt

False guilt is a common problem in adults and teens who have been victims of abuse or were blamed for everything by their parents and caregivers when they were children. Someone who is codependent may take responsibility for a partner's or parent's behavior. Someone who has unrealistic expectations of themselves may experience frequent bouts of guilt. What should we do when we feel guilty constantly?

First we must understand the root. Why are you feeling guilty? Your first question should be: Do I need to repent for something? Remember, guilt is a healthy negative emotion that protects relationships and builds our character. When you do something wrong, it is healthy to feel guilt. Godly sorrow will bring repentance (positive change), so identifying the root cause can go a long way in helping us process what we feel.

Are you experiencing guilt but don't want to repent? Let's say you were angry at your spouse and said something hurtful to her. You feel guilty, but you also feel that she deserved it. You may be experiencing worldly sorrow.

False guilt is different from either of these.

Are you experiencing guilt, but when you search your heart to repent you find nothing to repent for? This may be false guilt. Below is an example of this.

Gina was twenty-eight when she came to see me. She was recently married and they were very happy together. Prior to marrying Ethan, Gina had lived with her mother, Josie. Josie was a forty-eight-year-old single parent who was very dependent on Gina. Although Josie was very happy and supportive of her daughter's marriage, she often called Gina at all hours because she was lonely. Gina tried to set boundaries, but her mother would say things that made Gina feel guilty. Gina shared one recent episode:

> Ethan and I were snuggled on the couch watching a movie. It was almost 11:30. At first when the phone rang, I didn't answer it, but then I got worried, even though I had spent most of the day with my mom before Ethan got home from work. My mom was extremely concerned over the wind outside. She wanted me to come and look at a tree in

the backyard that was hitting the window. I knew it was of no concern. That tree always bumped against the window in the wind, and the wind was not particularly bad, so I told her I'd come over in the morning. That's when she told me I didn't care what happened to her. I only cared about myself now and hung up the phone! I tried to call her back, but she didn't answer, so I got ready to go over to check on her. I felt terrible. Ethan was clearly frustrated, and that's when I remembered what I had learned about false guilt. Did I need to repent? No. I am a dutiful, loving daughter and I actually spend a great deal of time with my mom and love her tons! When I stated this aloud, I realized that what I was feeling was false guilt.

The type of manipulation that Josie employed to incite guilt in her daughter was a product of unforgiveness. Even though Josie loved her daughter and wanted her to be happy, she carried unforgiveness toward her for getting married and leaving her alone. This may have grown out of her own loneliness and circumstances, but looking forward, if Josie is willing to identify this issue and repent, she will have a greater quality of life and a healthier relationship with her daughter.

False guilt is a negative, self-conscious emotion. It occurs when we cannot meet our own expectations, as in the case of not taking care of someone well enough or feeling responsible for things outside our control. If you feel guilt, ask yourself if you did something for which you need to repent. Discerning what's going on will help you take the next step.

It is important to understand the difference between real guilt that will lead to repentance, worldly sorrow, and false guilt (another negative, self-conscious emotion). Unhealthy negative emotions require people not only to consider themselves, but also require the ability to compare themselves to others. Self-conscious emotions grow out of an awareness of one's self compared to others as well as how one is perceived by others. For definition purposes, I have included a comprehensive excerpt from the article, "Guilty Feelings, Targeted Actions" below. I appreciate how the authors defined and differentiated guilt, shame, and regret in the excerpt below:

> Important distinctions between guilt and other negative self-conscious emotions exist. Regret occurs when a bad outcome is compared with a better outcome that could have resulted from different choices. In contrast, guilt occurs when a person feels responsible for a bad outcome that typically affected others (Zeelenberg & Breugelmans, 2008).[4] Shame occurs when someone feels bad about oneself for committing a transgression. In contrast, guilt occurs when a person feels bad about the transgression itself (Tangney, 1996).[5] These differences among the

4   Marcel Zeelenberg and Seger M. Breugelmans, "The Role of Interpersonal Harm in Distinguishing Regret from Guilt," *Emotion* 8, no. 5 (2008): pp. 589–596, https://doi.org/10.1037/a0012894.

5   June Price Tangney et al., "Are Shame, Guilt, and Embarrassment

origins of self-conscious emotions suggest unique consequences for the emotion of guilt. For example, whereas shame should produce withdrawal from social situations or broad attempts to correct one's status as a degraded person (de Hooge, Zeelenberg, & Breugelmans, 2007)[6], we expect guilt to prompt precise attempts to correct past transgressions.[7]

To summarize, guilt is a functional and healthy negative emotion that helps us evaluate our behavior and repent when we do something that hurts someone else. Since it's a healthy response, it's no surprise that the Bible supports it with its distinction between godly and worldly sorrow. We have a clear choice. When we are distressed about an outcome, we can choose to repent (turn around) and receive God's

> **Guilt is a functional and healthy negative emotion that helps us evaluate our behavior.**

divine grace. On the other hand, we can choose to ignore that option altogether, but if we do, we must remember that worldly sorrow leads to spiritual death. Because it is self-centered

---

Distinct Emotions?," *Journal of Personality and Social Psychology* 70, no. 6 (1996): pp. 1256–1269, https://doi.org/10.1037/0022–3514.70.6.1256.

6   J. P. Tangney and R. L. Dearing, "Shame and Guilt, Now and Then," *Shame and Guilt in Chaucer*, n.d., https://doi.org/10.1057/9781137039521.0003.

7   Ilona E. de Hooge, Marcel Zeelenberg, and Seger M. Breugelmans, "Moral Sentiments and Cooperation: Differential Influences of Shame and Guilt," *Cognition and Emotion* 21, no. 5 (2007): pp. 1025–1042, https://doi.org/10.1080/02699930600980874.

and self-absorbed, it is not conducive to real growth. If there is any expression of remorse in this case, it is the result of getting caught or in an effort to prevent negative consequences.

Additionally, false guilt occurs when we cannot meet our *own* expectations, as in the case of not taking care of someone well enough or feeling responsible for things outside our control. In every case, we need to pay attention to the effects of our behavior. We can choose to let godly sorrow lead us to repentance. If not, we may be sowing seeds of offense, which will bear the fruit of bitterness and unforgiveness in the future. Identifying what is going on is the necessary (and healthy) first step.

PRINCIPLE 5:
FORGIVENESS

> Make allowances for each
> other's faults, and forgive anyone
> who offends you. Remember, the
> Lord forgave you, so you must
> forgive others.
> (Colossians 3:13)

Proverbs tell us not to go to bed on our anger. We need to deal with offenses quickly. Consider poison ivy. If you are allergic to poison ivy and are exposed to it, you remove the culprit (urushiol oil) from your skin as fast as you can. Time is of the essence. You run for the soap and scrub the exposed areas. You take no chances and scrub areas that may have been near the exposed area, and put your clothing in the wash too, just in case. When you know in advance that you might be around poison ivy, you dress accordingly, wearing gloves, long pants, and heavy socks. You don't fool around about it, but take the necessary steps to ensure that the urushiol oil does not cause an outbreak. There is no delay in your response without consequence.

We need to treat offenses this way too.

And "don't sin by letting anger control you." Don't let the sun go down while you are still angry. (Ephesians 4:26)

Why shouldn't we let the sun go down on our anger? Because it evolves and changes into something else overnight. Have you ever had an argument with your spouse before bed and went to sleep without resolving the issue? You might wake without strong feelings in the light of a new day, but the seed of offense was planted and the problem is unresolved. Until it is dealt with, it will continue to grow, entangling itself with any part of your mind with which it can possibly connect. In the darkness of our minds (and our minds can be pretty dark), we all cultivate our own garden. Its plants grow quickly, often morphing into fruit that seems to bear little resemblance to the original seed. In our dark garden, we can grow fear, anxiety and depression, all rooted in offenses. How do we prevent this? Hold short accounts. Address offenses when they occur as much as possible. Jesus taught this: "If your brother sins against you, go and tell him his fault, between you and him alone. If he listens to you, you have gained your brother" (Matt. 18:15 ESV).

It took me a while to learn this. On one occasion, some of my friends were offended with me. I knew they were offended and waited for them to come to me, but they didn't right away. Because I wasn't the one who was offended, I thought it was not my responsibility to resolve it. However, Jesus clearly taught that it was as much my responsibility to go to them as it was for them to come to me. Because I waited for them to come to me, that offense was allowed to fester into bitterness. How did it end?

Holding short accounts means there is no delay in my response when an offense occurs, regardless which party we are: the sinner or the person being sinned against. This is a very important principle. Jesus said this:

> So if you are presenting a sacrifice at the altar in the Temple and you suddenly remember that someone has something against you, leave your sacrifice there at the altar. Go and be reconciled to that person. Then come and offer your sacrifice to God. (Matthew 5:23–24)

We are responsible if we know someone has a problem with us. Short accounts are the answer to dealing with this. Not only is it part of our thinking in dealing with poison ivy and people, but it's also how we run a business. As a counselor, I often receive co-pays from my clients. I am pretty flexible if someone forgets their co-pay at times, but I learned years ago to hold short

We are responsible if we know someone has a problem with us.

accounts, and not let someone accumulate a large debt of co-pays. I had a patient who got into the habit of paying their collective co-pay when the total reached around $200.00! The weekly co-pay was $15.00! They always paid me, but it became uncomfortable as each week the tradition of requesting this co-pay became part of our conversation. It was always cordial;

they were not trying to get out of paying; but the more the unpaid bill accumulated, the more stressful requesting the co-pay became on my end. After she was discharged from counseling, I no longer allowed this as a general practice.

When we do not keep short accounts, we create fertile ground for a seed of offense to sprout and grow. This happened in my life when I was a new Christian just beginning in ministry, and I lost a very important relationship as a result. At the time, I was a supervisor over a very close friend. Because of my own frustration and burnout, I was not able to support her when she really needed help. I did not realize that my actions were as damaging as they were, and although I apologized, I didn't repent and seek forgiveness. *An apology is an expression of remorse. It is not repentance.* This doesn't mean a sincere apology is unimportant. It just means that the apology itself is not repentance. When you repent you make positive changes in your life. For example, if someone cheats on their spouse, they can be remorseful about the act, but repentance happens when the individual makes the necessary changes to be faithful to his or her spouse going forward.

In the case of my friend, over time our friendship changed drastically. We grew apart. Although I was still included in major celebrations and family affairs, I had no other connection with her. She left the ministry and I carried on. Bitterness and resentment set in and unforgiveness began growing in the dark garden. As I grew in my understanding, I often tried to reach out to her. I enjoyed our time together, but once we parted ways, she never called me. I had to be the one to reach out.

I didn't understand at the time how manipulation followed unforgiveness. When I look back, I think we both felt justified, but both of us were operating in manipulation. She never shared her hurt with me, or the fact that she still harbored negative feelings toward me. And I didn't ask. We went on periodically engaging with one another, but not really. Most of the time, we waded through our lives without each other.

Some form of manipulation often follows unforgiveness. Think about the times you have struggled to forgive someone. Chances are you've engaged in some form of manipulation as a result. We all have.

Manipulation may look like any of the following. (This is far from a complete list, but I am only writing one book!)

- Avoidance through ghosting, blocking, not showing up, or using the silent treatment.
- Gossip, sometimes in the form of prayer or social media posts, such as, "Father, please help Sarah stop hurting people with her lies..." or a cryptic post, like this one: "Please pray for me. Someone is really trying to bring drama into my life after...." I once had someone who was offended with me call me periodically to apologize because she had slandered me in conversations with other people and wanted my forgiveness. (This was long after she initially became offended with me.) *Malicious gossip is a powerful tool of the Enemy.*
- Embarrassing, shaming, or humiliating someone.
- Not following through with commitments.
- Use of sarcasm or insults.

Some of this happens without unforgiveness. There's the potential for manipulation in any situation in which someone feels the need to be in control due to feelings of hurt, abandonment, rejection, or insecurity. It is likely that these feelings come from unforgiveness. Sometimes, offenses are so old that they grow cold, and a person no longer recognizes that they are harboring unforgiveness. Also, keep in mind that someone can be harboring unforgiveness toward another, but not you. Think about Joe who is in a relationship with Aubrey, and had had two earlier serious relationships in which both women had cheated on him and later left. Joe entered this relationship guarded and filled with insecurity. He was harboring a lot of pain and unforgiveness, but not toward Aubrey. In fact, he really cared for Aubrey. The unforgiveness existed before he met her, along with its accompanying insecurity and fear of abandonment. Although he never intended to hurt Aubrey, they came for counseling because of communication issues. In his effort to elicit particular responses, Joe was being manipulative. Psychological manipulation can be defined as "the exercise of undue influence through mental distortion and emotional exploitation, with the intention to seize power, control, benefits and/or privileges at the victim's expense."[8]

Joe wasn't trying to hurt Aubrey, but his lack of trust and insecurities governed how he chose his words. One day, Joe walked in on Aubrey speaking on the phone with a male

---

8   Preston Ni, "14 Signs of Psychological and Emotional Manipulation," *Psychology Today* (Sussex Publishers), accessed June 22, 2022, https://www.psychologytoday.com/us/blog/communication-success/201510/14–signs-psychological-and-emotional-manipulation.

colleague discussing a deadline. Even though Joe heard nothing that should have triggered his mistrust, and he knew Ray, her colleague, when the phone conversation ended, Joe became a bit distant and said, "Ray has it together. I feel bad you are stuck with me when you could have someone like that." Immediately, Aubrey felt guilty (false guilt) and began to reassure Joe. Aubrey thought she needed to defend an innocent exchange, and also cut Ray down a bit to help Joe feel more secure. This behavior resulted in discomfort later when she came in contact with Ray at the office. Aubrey shared that she never considered Ray in any way other than a colleague. They both shared that her behavior was consistent with this, but the phone call triggered Joe and reminded him of times when he had walked in on conversations between his ex-girlfriends and the other men they had been seeing.

Manipulation is erosive. In a case like this, the innocent party struggles to continue to defend their honor and grows weary. This particularly happens when, early on, the person being manipulated provides reassurance, support, and security in response to the manipulation. Aubrey's feedback made Joe feel safe and so he sought it regularly. The positive feedback she gave prolonged Joe's need as well. After five months—when it became apparent to Aubrey how this worked—Aubrey started rolling her eyes and shutting down instead of offering reassurance. This, in turn, just fed Joe's underlying insecurities.

What was the remedy? Obviously, Joe needed to work through the feelings and insecurities he had brought into the relationship; but first and foremost, the manipulation had to end. We began infusing direct and truthful communication into the conversation. When Joe needed reassurance, he needed to honestly ask for it. Aubrey would support him in this need only when it was directly communicated. Additionally, when Joe felt insecure, he began to share that with her by saying things, like, "Aubrey, I am having thoughts that make me feel insecure. You are not responsible for these thoughts, I know, but they are present." Sometimes they then discussed his thoughts, and sometimes it helped Joe to simply inform Aubrey about them. Either way, the thoughts lost their power over Joe in time. They lost some power immediately after he shared how he felt. Once they were vocalized directly, they were taken out of the darkness of Joe's mind and into the light which diminished their power.

Manipulation is considered sorcery in the Bible. In Acts 8, we are introduced to Simon the Sorcerer. He wanted to buy the gift of healing when he saw the disciples healing and leading people to Christ. In the *New Spirit-Filled Life Bible* note for Acts 8:23, it says:

> Peter identified the basis for Simon's sorcery as bitterness—the deepening effect of unforgiveness (v. 2). Here is warning regarding the danger of tolerated or embraced unforgiveness, which may, like poison, permeate and bind the soul, ultimately corrupting everything around it. In Simon's case, his bitterness shaped his passion to control others (v. 19)—which prompted his quest to purchase the ability to impart the gift of the Holy Spirit. Though having believed and been baptized (v.

13), the residue of his past bondage surfaces as he unworthily seeks power to manipulate others for self-exalting purposes. Peter discerns the root of his bondage (v. 23) and summons Simon to repentance and deliverance. Though Simon did not repent, this episode still points to one of the foremost keys to deliverance from entrenched bondage in a believer's soul—the act of forgiveness. Forgiving others from our heart flushes out the "poison" with the power of the Cross. In contrast, unforgiveness can, as with Simon, lead down paths we would never have imagined we would travel.[9]

Bitterness

What else can we do to forgive? We talked about holding short accounts. Here are some other ways to help facilitate forgiveness.

Pray blessings over a person who offended you. Pray earnestly for them and pray for the blessings that you would want to receive if you were them. Pray for them regularly.

Look at the baggage people are carrying. Where did it come from? My pastor shared this in a sermon several years ago and it really resonated with me. *Hurting people hurt people.* This accounts for so many offenses. Understanding the hurt of those that hurt you helps. It is easier to forgive people when you look at the hand they were dealt, and their subsequent

---

9 Jack W. Hayford, Paul Chappell, and Kenneth C. Ulmer, *New Spirit-Filled Life Bible* (Nashville: Thomas Nelson, 2015).

struggles. Forgiveness comes easier when you have compassion and mercy for someone.

Forgiving someone does not give them a license to hurt you again. Some people hold on to unforgiveness because they feel that if they forgive, they will be hurt again. They think they are protecting themselves somehow. This logic is untrue. Having forgiveness in your heart does not rationally correlate to someone hurting you again. You can forgive someone earnestly *and* have good boundaries, but they are two very separate things.

Understand that apologizing is not the same as seeking forgiveness. An apology is an expression of remorse. A sincere, heartfelt apology is a step in the process of forgiveness. It's important, but it is only one step.

Forgiveness is a choice requiring premeditation.

Be intentional. Forgiveness is a choice requiring premeditation.

Keep pride in check. Isaiah 23:9 tells us that God resists the proud in order to show them their need of Him. I always tell people that pride is an "earthly protection." We should be seeking godly protection instead. Pride is a way to protect our feelings. It can prevent forgiveness from happening. Our pride can allow so much time to pass that the offense is removed from your mind or justified, instead of being properly handled. Pride can also justify a sense of entitlement. People who feel entitled often do not forgive or feel that they need to be forgiven. They have trouble apologizing or genuinely seeking forgiveness.

Jesus Christ made us blameless when He died for us on the cross. If someone is blameless, there is nothing to forgive. This may seem radical. It may even upset you. After all, where is the justice in that? Ask Jesus. Where was the justice in *that?* All the blame for everyone was placed on Him. In exchange, we receive mercy.

PRINCIPLE 6:
THE ENTITLEMENT COMPLEX

Now such persons we command
and encourage in the Lord Jesus
Christ to do their work quietly
and to earn their own living.
(2 Thessalonians 3:12 ESV)

I predominantly work with low-income people. I frequently hear about how entitled people are. This concept is applied to different social groups. The term *entitled* commonly refers to when someone feels and asserts that they have a right to be treated a certain special way by others. Most of the people that fit this definition are people between the ages of sixteen and thirty-five from middle- and upper-middle-class families. Having a sense of entitlement is a very dangerous mindset to have. Let's look at it more closely.

Casey was a nineteen-year-old freshman at a four-year college. She was struggling to have acceptable grades, and was angry and depressed much of the time. She lived with her grandparents, who became concerned about her depression and anger and asked her to see me.

We began going through her history and discussing her depression. Some things were notable right off the bat. First, she shared that she was living with her aging grandparents because her mom wouldn't let her have boys spend the night. She stated that her grandparents were trying to get her to move out of their house, but she wasn't going to leave. When Casey had a boy at the house and they opposed this and asked that he leave, Casey was verbally abusive and withheld favors. She also refused to have the boy leave, making the grandparents feel uncomfortable and fearful. Casey also paid no rent and had free use of their only vehicle, even though she was not working. The most striking thing about this is that she felt that she deserved everything her grandparents did for her. She had no remorse about any of her actions, and felt she was not doing anything wrong. She was angry when her grandparents would not give in to her demands.

Casey was doing poorly in school because she did not want to be there. She found the work boring, and was much more interested in the social aspects of school. She attended classes, but did not complete assignments.

She truly enjoyed counseling. She enjoyed talking about herself and having one-on-one time that was dedicated completely to her. I had to pray for grace before she came in. Her entitled behavior and complete disregard for others was difficult to deal with.

However, it is important to understand that Casey really was depressed. Her entitlement complex contributed to a vicious cycle that often manifested in anger and depression. She was typically miserable. Her grandparents could retreat to their room when she made demands, but her peers and professors were not so inclined. For instance, disappointment and hurt feelings quickly manifested when her idea for a group project was rejected by the rest of her classmates. These hurt feelings led to anger. Casey began to oppose any suggestions made by the others out of hand. Her anger was noticeable, and her behavior was producing obstacles to project completion. Of course, she felt it was the group's fault for not putting her in charge of the visual presentation as she had initially requested. She was denied that position because there was another member of the group whose major gave him a better background, giving the group a better chance at a good grade.

A 2016 study at the University of Hampshire conducted by Dr. Joshua Grubbs found that people with an entitlement complex have unmet expectations in many areas of their lives and are likely to experience disappointment or ego threat. Such individuals are more easily offended and often blame others for unjust treatment.[10]

Our society and culture has changed a great deal just in my lifetime. Currently in my fifties, I have the opportunity to help people learn from the many mistakes I have made in parenting, relationships, and other areas of my life. From my vantage point, I believe placating has taken on a whole new role in our society and culture, and contributes greatly to the development

---

10 Joshua B. Grubbs and Julie J. Exline, "Trait Entitlement: A Cognitive-Personality Source of Vulnerability to Psychological Distress," *Psychological Bulletin* 142, no. 11 (2016): pp. 1204–1226, https://doi.org/10.1037/bul0000063.

of an entitlement complex. Unfortunately, we sometimes placate feelings and call it diplomacy.

To *placate* is "to appease or pacify" or mollify.[11] The term *mollify* means "to soften or appease."[12] Mollifying typically refers to pacifying someone who is perhaps angry or anxious. Placating by itself is not a bad thing. Sometimes it is necessary. However, our busy lifestyles have meddled with having the time to really connect with people the way we ought, so placating has become a common problem solving tool. Unfortunately, it is not without its own problems.

When society becomes more concerned with how people feel rather than how they behave, the seed for an entitlement complex is planted.

When somebody yells, disrupts, cries, is agitated or angry, placating happens without always discovering the root of the problem or seeking true resolution. This is not a criticism. Just an observation. We are so busy and there is so much to do and so much stimulation that we seek the quickest and easiest way to solve a problem. It's a natural tendency.

In an earlier chapter, we discussed the outcomes we wanted to achieve in our interactions with others. When society becomes more concerned with how people feel rather than how they behave, the seed for an entitlement complex is planted. I

11 "Placate Definition & Meaning," *Webster's Unabridged Dictionary*, part of the public domain at Project Gutenberg..

12 "Mollify Definition & Meaning," *Webster's Unabridged Dictionary*, part of the public domain at Project Gutenberg.

am not saying we should disregard people's emotions. Emotions are important indicators. I am saying that when we cover deep wounds with a bandage, we are perpetuating (and possibly increasing) behavior associated with negative emotions.

Consider this example: Christopher had been coming to the Victory Warming Shelter for a while. He was a homeless individual with an addiction, but did not want any help with his addiction problem. He was often rude to the people caring for him, and caused disturbances, speaking unkindly to the café staff preparing his meal. Perhaps he behaved this way to get particular food, or maybe he was struggling because he was experiencing withdrawal symptoms, or he just hurt others because he was so hurt himself. Whichever it was, the café worker's aim was to maintain peace and end the confrontational behavior. She told Christopher that she would make him what he asked for if he sat down and was polite and respectful.

You might think she was showing grace, but it is important to recognize that when the negative behaviors are patterned, this kind of "grace" had been negatively reinforced and happened frequently. Additionally, the meal (or other reward) did not fill the emptiness that Christopher's emotions reflected. This made her soothing words of very temporary effect. It didn't necessarily start out that way though. Christopher's emotions were real and indicated what he was experiencing. At some point, he had learned he would be rewarded intermittently when he displayed negative behavior.

Emotions are important, God-given qualities that act as indicators of an individual's state of being. Remember the analogy about a car's indicator lights? If the engine light on the dashboard goes on, it doesn't mean that the engine light is responsible for a problem with the engine. The light merely alerts us to the problem that *already exists* in the engine.

Let's talk about John now. John was a high school student who missed so many classes that he failed his English class. His parents came in for a conference with the teacher, a school social worker, and the principal. John's parents were angry at the teacher and blamed her for their son's lack of success. John bore no responsibility for skipping 60% of his classes! Instead, the teacher got lambasted and received no support from her principal or the social worker. She left the meeting feeling defeated. Not only did John receive no consequences for his behavior, he witnessed the lack of support for his teacher, which strengthened his feelings of power and self-righteousness. For John, the seed was planted long before this.

When he was four, John's parents divorced. He lived primarily with his mother and stepfather. It didn't take long for John to witness his mother's intervention when Eric, John's stepdad, tried to discipline him. His mother would yell at her husband and explain John's motivation for his bad behavior, often blaming her ex-husband (John's father) for the behavior. John learned at a young age that he did not have to respect authority. Instead, he could manipulate situations easily through expressions of sadness, hurt, and anger whenever he was behaving badly.

An entitlement complex in an individual looks like narcissism. Most of the people I have counseled that had an entitlement mentality were frequently disappointed, felt they were wronged by those around them, were often easily offended, and viewed criticism as a threat. They often presented as being "unteachable" and lacked humility.[13]

The cycle is simple. Here's an example: (1) I deserve to make a lot of money. (2) I have an entry level job because I am new to the workforce, but I deserve a promotion and to be making more money. (3) Disappointment sets in. (4) That disappointment mixed with a mounting frustration grows because I am not a humble employee, and am sure I deserve more. (5) I complain to my coworkers, appear disgruntled, and am often critical. (6) I get reprimanded for my attitude at work. (7) I am angry and feel the action was unjust. (8) This escalates until I lose the job. *Everything was so unfair!* (9) I find another job and tell myself that my former employer didn't deserve anyone like me. I reassure myself that I was a great employee and they undervalued me. (10) The cycle begins again.

An entitlement complex is detrimental to our relationships and very destructive in the lives of the entitled one as well as all those around them. Viewing the world through a narcissistic lens leads to anger, depression, and anxiety. People with entitlement complexes tend to have a reduced quality of life as they battle through the cycle. The act of constantly reassuring themselves that they are deserving is exhausting and leads to greater degrees of anger, depression, and disappointment over time.[8] In an article entitled, "16 Signs You Might Have an Entitlement Complex," Aletheia Luna refers to entitlement

---

13 Joshua B. Grubbs and Julie J. Exline, "Trait Entitlement: A Cognitive-Personality Source of Vulnerability to Psychological Distress," *Psychological Bulletin* 142, no. 11 (2016): pp. 1204–1226, https://doi.org/10.1037/bul0000063.

complex as a "malignant form of self-love" because it is so harmful to our friends, families, and ultimately ourselves.[14]

It is easy to see symptoms of entitlement complex in the homeless and those living in poverty. I've often heard people say that the homeless or poor don't want to work. They just want to sponge off the system. I don't think that is true.

When we only look at a symptom and not the condition, we can easily misjudge. Take a sneeze for example. Sneezing could be a symptom of allergies, flu, a cold, COVID-19, or something situational, such as breathing in a little black pepper while you are grinding it. Each of these conditions requires different care and treatment; but if we only look at the sneezing, we could easily get the diagnosis wrong, and therefore prescribe the wrong treatment which could be harmful or worsen the condition.

This is very true of learned helplessness. Learned helplessness can sometimes look like an entitlement complex, while entitlement is a symptom of learned helplessness, which we will consider next.

---

14 Aletheia Luna, "16 Signs You Have a Sense of Entitlement Complex," Awakening People, accessed June 22, 2022, https://www.awakeningpeople. com/16–signs-you-have-a-sense-of-entitlement-complex.html.

PRINCIPLE 7:
LEARNED HELPLESSNESS

> Don't be afraid, for I am with you.
> Don't be discouraged, for I am
> your God. I will strengthen you
> and help you. I will hold you up
> with my victorious right hand.
> (Isaiah 41:10)

Learned helplessness looks a lot like entitlement, but even though it shares similar characteristics, it is quite different. In 1967, research was being conducted that involved delivering electric shocks to dogs. When the dogs learned that they couldn't escape getting shocked, they stopped trying—even when they could jump over a barrier to avoid getting shocked.

Learned helplessness occurs when a person experiences repeated negative situations that are out of his or her control. Eventually, the individual stops trying to change things, even when he or she is able to do so. Baby Elephant Syndrome is a good example. Imagine a baby elephant in the circus. The trainer ties a baby elephant securely to a pole. The little elephant will try to break free, but cannot. Then the trainer removes the rope temporarily and puts it back. The baby elephant again struggles to break free, but is unable. Eventually the rope itself is enough to keep the baby elephant captive, even if loosely tied. The elephant has recognized its helplessness. It knows it cannot get free when tied.

Baby Elephant Syndrome happens to people too. I have counseled many adult survivors of sexual or physical abuse as children who have this same sense of powerlessness. Survivors of domestic violence and those subject to incessant bullying also deal with this. Frequently the theme in many of these situations is that the individual *really was powerless* to help him or herself. However, even when someone knows intellectually that he or she has the power to positively impact a situation now, core beliefs cement them in the belief that he or she is helpless instead.

It is my experience that in matters between the heart and head, the heart wins. I worked with a man in his fifties who had a history of trauma and mental health issues. He had been severely bullied in school. By ninth grade, Lonnie was 6' 1" with a stocky build. He could have easily prevented the bullying and teasing with his intimidating stature, but he didn't. He didn't even try. Instead, he avoided school; he was truant more often than not and dropped out of school in the tenth grade.

Learned helplessness often appears similar to an entitlement complex. I see it frequently in the individuals I work with in ministry. I was counseling Wes and Mary. Wes was unemployed and Mary worked at a big box department store. They first came for help with housing and had been housing-vulnerable for much of their relationship. They were currently in the process of being evicted. In counseling, we looked at some of the factors that led to their housing situation. Wes struggled to get a job and had a scant employment history. After a few months at one of the four jobs he had, he would need to quit for some health-related reason. Wes was obese, but appeared otherwise healthy. He was intelligent, but often depressed and quite pessimistic. He had an argument for why he couldn't do something before he was even asked about doing it. This was creating many problems in the couple's marriage. Mary was unable to make enough money to support them both as she only had a part-time job. Wes' behavior was eroding their relationship.

One day the couple came to therapy and Wes seemed particularly down. He shared that he had a big argument with his mom and sister. Apparently, they questioned him as to why he was not collecting Supplemental Security Income (SSI) through Social Security to support his family. Both his sister and mother were on SSI. Wes stated that he felt like a loser because he had not begun the application process yet. He knew intellectually that most people worked to support their families, but his core belief was that he needed to be on SSI to support his family. He didn't think he could be a provider in his own home.

This is a face of learned helplessness. We see this frequently in families who receive public assistance and were raised on public assistance. Many think these folks have an entitlement complex and feel they deserve a free ride, but this is not the case. Often, learned helplessness can be entitling—not because someone feels they *deserve* something, but because someone perceives that his or her survival *depends* on it. It is what they know and what they were taught. Wes grew up in a household that did not promote employment as the means to take care of one's self or family. He grew up with a core belief that he could only be an adequate provider if he received public benefits, even though intellectually he knew that people worked to provide for themselves and their families.

So how do you overcome learned helplessness? *Learned optimism is the opposite of learned helplessness.*[15] Martin E. P. Seligman founded Positive Psychology in the 1990s to focus more on well-being as opposed to sickness. Seligman's book, *Learned Optimism*, teaches people to cultivate optimism through changing the framework in which they view situations. According to Seligman, "Changing the destructive things you say to yourself when you experience the setbacks that life deals all of us is the central skill of optimism."[16]

All people experience setbacks and failures. Some people get through their setbacks and move on. Others may personalize and make the setback permanent and pervasive, taking away hope. Karen was a thirty-four–year-old mother of two who came to me in crisis because her boyfriend of eleven months abruptly ended their relationship and started dating another woman. Karen stated that this happened to her "all the time." Her framework for looking at this breakup gives her no hope of ever having a good relationship. If it happens

---

15 Martin E. Seligman and Steven F. Maier, "Failure to Escape Traumatic Shock," *Journal of Experimental Psychology* 74, no. 1 (1967): pp. 1–9, https://doi.org/10.1037/h0024514.

16 Martin E. P. Seligman, *Learned Optimism: How to Change Your Mind and Your Life* (New York: Vintage Books, 2006).

all the time (permanence and pervasiveness), there is no hope for change.

Karen believed she was not a good girlfriend and had a hard time balancing her roles as a mom, employee, and being in a relationship. She also felt unworthy. Although she intellectually understood that she was not responsible for her father leaving, her core belief was that if she would have been a better daughter, he would have stayed. Her father and mother had separated when she was nine, and she was still carrying that perspective into her relationships.

According to Seligman, if you explain a failure permanently and pervasively, that failure becomes the standard for all future situations. Since Karen perceived that *all* relationships turned out this way because she was not good enough, her thinking was both permanent and pervasive.[17]

Counseling Karen involved reframing this belief. Instead of looking at herself as unworthy, we explored the fact that her low self-esteem led her into relationships with men that exploited her lack of self-worth. We also worked on building her confidence and self-esteem. One exercise we did was to look at each "significant" relationship she had had in the past (Karen defined significant), and explore the evidence contrary to her pervasive and permanent explanations of each relationship's eventual demise.

Now let's look at Wes' beliefs in the previous example. Wes believed a script that told him the only way to be successful and take care of your family was through government support.

---

17 Ibid.

Even though he *knew* intellectually that he could work, his core (or heart) belief was that he could not work and had to go on disability to have a steady income.

I see manifestations of learned helplessness every day. The public assistance benefit system is often difficult to get out of with upward mobility. If people have medical needs or get a job that pays minimum wage, losing insurance and inadequate gap coverage make it difficult to transition out of the system. This can easily look like an entitlement complex. Unfortunately, when we look at these individuals as entitled, we do not provide the effective encouragement and supportive intervention they need so they can overcome this barrier to self-sufficiency.

Many times we need to work through the entitled behavior to get to the root of the learned helplessness.

I am of the opinion that the easiest way to distinguish whether someone is operating from a mindset of learned helplessness versus an entitlement complex is just to sit and talk with the person. Get to know them. Ask them "why" a lot. Develop a history. With learned helplessness, entitlement is a coping mechanism—one people don't even recognize within themselves because they have been conditioned to believe the lies that they are not able, not worthy, or not enough. Many times we need to work through the entitled behavior to get to the root of the learned helplessness.

In either case, both are suffering. Entitlement often comes off with an air of pride or arrogance, but those experiencing it are hurt, insecure, and feeling rejected and unworthy. Gratitude and humility are the tools for change that they need. Gratitude is the lens that magnifies optimism and all positive emotions. We need to intentionally teach this to our young, and continue those lessons throughout life.

PRINCIPLE 8:
HUMILITY AND GRATITUDE

Do nothing from selfish ambition
or conceit, but in humility count
others more significant than
yourselves. Let each of you look
not only to his own interests, but
also to the interests of others.
(Philippians 2:3–4 ESV)

Be thankful in all circumstances,
for this is God's will for you who
belong to Christ Jesus.
(1 Thessalonians 5:18)

The cure for entitlement complex is humility and gratitude. This does not mean that a humble person views himself as being without worth and value. The definition of *humility* is "freedom from pride or arrogance,"[18] so a humble person is modest and does not have an exaggerated view of their own im-

---

18 "Humility Definition & Meaning," *Webster's Unabridged Dictionary,* part of the public domain at Project Gutenberg.

portance. Humility is *hypoegoic* in Greek. *Hypo* means "under"[19] and *ego* literally means ego.[20] The ego is basically our "self." A person with humility is more social and values others more. They are more likely to find happiness in others and have better quality relationships and more of them. Examples of humility would include someone who cleans the bathroom at his workplace, even though he is the owner. The inverse of this would be the owner who felt cleaning bathrooms was beneath him, and insisted that an overworked staff member clean them immediately.

A grateful heart that shouts appreciation combats entitlement.

Another example could be a football player who credits the team with the win, even though he has great skill and aptitude, instead of being the guy who is always bragging to everyone that he carries the team.

What is the "cure" for entitlement complex? It is simple, but takes plenty of time and a willingness to learn. Gratitude is the cure for entitlement. A grateful heart that shouts appreciation combats entitlement. A paper entitled "An Upward Spiral between Gratitude and Humility" looked at the relationship between gratitude and humility and determined that gratitude and humility were mutually reinforcing. According to their studies, people experiencing and practicing gratitude valued

---

19 James Strong, "G5259 - Hypo - Strong's Greek Lexicon (KJV)," Blue Letter Bible, accessed July 5, 2022, https://www.blueletterbible.org/lexicon/g5259/kjv/tr/0–1/.

20 James Strong, "G1473 - Egō - Strong's Greek Lexicon (KJV)," Blue Letter Bible, accessed July 5, 2022, https://www.blueletterbible.org/lexicon/g1473/kjv/tr/0–1/.

others and naturally would be less focused on themselves, leading to humility. Additionally, people who were humble were more accepting of the good in other people and valued them more, making them more grateful still.[21]

The Bible teaches much about gratitude. First Thessalonians 5:18 tells us to "give thanks in all circumstances; for this is God's will for you in Christ Jesus" (NIV). Gratitude is an important biblical principle. Let's look closely at this concept. You might be thinking to yourself, *I know what gratitude is. I don't need to consider it further.* Nevertheless, let's do it anyway.

Gratitude is an expression of appreciation. When we experience gratitude it comes from within, but the *act* of being grateful is a conscious, intentional choice. After clinical experiences with entitled people who are miserable (and some who may be experiencing suicidal ideation due to feeling rejected when their entitlement is challenged), I believe that a curriculum of gratitude should be taught in schools as well as churches. A famous quote by Ralph Waldo Emerson sums it up well: "Cultivate the habit of being grateful for every good thing that comes to you, and to give thanks continuously. And because all things have contributed to your advancement, you should include all things in your gratitude."[22]

---

21 Elliott Kruse et al., "An Upward Spiral between Gratitude and Humility," *Social Psychological and Personality Science* 5, no. 7 (2014): pp. 805–814, https://doi.org/10.1177/1948550614534700.

22 Ralph Waldo Emerson, "A Quote by Ralph Waldo Emerson," Goodreads (Goodreads), accessed July 5, 2022, https://www.goodreads.com/quotes/14132–cultivate-the-habit-of-being-grateful-for-every-good-thing.

That quote addresses the belief that everything we have—including our lives—is a gift. In the past decade, research has looked at the health benefits of gratitude in addition to its social and psychological benefits. Genuine appreciation and gratitude is healing, enhances relationships, contributes to our physical health, and wards off depression and other mental health concerns.

So how do we define gratitude? Robert Emmons and Michael McCullough define gratitude as a two-step process: 1) "recognizing that one has obtained a positive outcome" and 2) "recognizing that there is an external source for this positive outcome."[23] What does this mean? Here is a very simple example. I have some beautiful friends and congregations that sow into our outreach ministry financially. Recently we acquired a building through auction that will serve as our ministry's new home.

Victory did a GoFundMe page and a letter writing campaign to get help with this acquisition. The outpouring of support overwhelmed me. First, I recognized that Victory had obtained a positive outcome through this outpouring of financial support. Second, I recognized that emotions welled up within me as I recognized the love and generosity of these beautiful people. The second part happens every time I think about this outpouring and it happens to the people I am grateful for whenever I express my gratitude to them. It's a healing cycle.

---

23   Robert A. Emmons and Michael E. McCullough, "Counting Blessings versus Burdens: An Experimental Investigation of Gratitude and Subjective Well-Being in Daily Life," *Journal of Personality and Social Psychology* 84, no. 2 (2003): pp. 377–389, https://doi.org/10.1037/0022–3514.84.2.377.

Why is this framework important? It clearly illustrates that gratitude is both a disposition (inherent qualities) and a state of being (quality of one's present experience), giving it exponential positive power. I shop at Aldi frequently, and participate in what I refer to as my "quarter ministry." This consists of me leaving my cart for another shopper with the quarter still in it. This is a conscious choice and so is the desire to do it. I get great pleasure out of giving gifts. I love feeling grateful and would like everyone to experience this. When I walk up to the store, particularly on those days when I can't find a quarter, seeing a cart up by the door ready for my use is so gratifying. This simple act of kindness can influence my attitude for the rest of the day. And then I have the privilege of paying the cart forward!

People who practice and experience gratitude are less stressed, happier, have better relationships, and better physical health. When we are practicing and experiencing gratitude, we are changing the world in a positive way.[24] Positive thoughts and experiences create a positive heart; and out of the heart, the mouth speaks (Luke 6:45). Positive words can affect the chemistry and stress levels of the people around you too. Grateful people share! This is part of the premise of the Broaden-and-Build Theory by Barbara L. Fredrickson. Broaden-and-Build Theory depicts

> **People who practice and experience gratitude are less stressed, happier, have better relationships, and better physical health.**

24 Ibid.

positive emotions as being necessary for optimal functioning. The theory suggests that positive emotions expand attention, undo effects of negative emotion, and promote resiliency. Positive emotions build people up and help people grow more positive. We all need to intentionally cultivate positive emotions in our day-to-day living.[25]

Humility and gratitude grow each other and have numerous physical, mental, and social health benefits. Numerous Bible references, as well as articles and scientific studies show the benefits of these qualities in an individual.

Now let's explore some other states and traits such as fear, anxiety, and anger, and look at both the good and bad aspects of these characteristics.

---

25 Barbara L. Fredrickson, "The Broaden–and–Build Theory of Positive Emotions," *Philosophical Transactions of the Royal Society of London. Series B: Biological Sciences* 359, no. 1449 (2004): pp. 1367–1377, https://doi.org/10.1098/rstb.2004.1512.

PRINCIPLE 9:
ANGER, THE STUNT DOUBLE

> Understand this, my dear brothers
> and sisters: You must all be quick
> to listen, slow to speak, and slow
> to get angry. Human anger does
> not produce the righteousness
> God desires.
> (James 1:19–20)

Let's start with an offense. I am taking my friend Jennifer out to lunch. We have agreed to meet at a particular restaurant, but I forgot and didn't show up. I did not intend to be careless with my friend's feelings. I overbooked. This is the seed. I can just envision it as a dark seed that has been planted. Jennifer is offended and angry. I wasted her time.

Since anger is a big part of example, let's break it down a little. As a noun, the standard definition for *anger* is "a strong passion or emotion of displeasure or antagonism."[26] Here are common synonyms for *anger*: wrath, ire, rage, dander, fury, annoyance, and irritation. I don't look at anger this way.

26 "Anger Definition & Meaning," *Webster's Unabridged Dictionary*, part of the public domain at Project Gutenberg.

Consider anger as a secondary emotion. I liken it to a stunt double. Chris Hemsworth, who plays Thor in the Marvel Cinematic Universe (MCU), uses a stunt double to do most of his stunts. I don't blame him a bit; Thor is in some pretty crazy scenes. When it is time for Thanos to hurl him into a tree that breaks on impact in *Avengers: Endgame*, someone says, "Cut," and his highly trained stunt double comes in to perform the dangerous part of the stunt.

That is what anger does. When someone has to feel one of those yucky emotions, like humiliation, embarrassment, worry, or hurt—sometimes anger gets called in. Anger is powerful, and can handle the stunt quickly and easily. Some people call in anger before the primary, negative emotion gets a chance to manifest. This happens frequently, especially when we have repeatedly experienced negative emotions that make us feel vulnerable like rejection, or when an angry response was modeled for us by parents or older siblings.

Anger is a healthy, God-given emotion.

Why is there so much power in anger? Anger is a healthy, God-given emotion. There is nothing wrong with anger as an emotion. A part of the brain called the amygdala helps coordinate responses to things in your environment, especially things that trigger an emotional response. The amygdala is best known for its role in processing fear; and it is so effective that it can often trigger a fear response before we even know we are afraid.[27] In addition to its involvement in the initiation of

27 Arne Öhman et al., "On the Unconscious Subcortical Origin of Human Fear," *Physiology & Behavior* 92, no. 1–2 (2007): pp. 180–185, https://

a fear response, the amygdala also seems to be very important in forming memories that are associated with fear-inducing events. This may help us understand anxiety and anxiety disorders. Fear is a response to a threat; anxiety is dread and concern over a threat that has yet to happen or a threat that may not even be real.[28] Much like fear, anger is a response to threats or stressors in your environment. Consider that anger is like the "fight" part of fight or flight. *Anger provides responsive power.*

We've discussed why anger would present itself when someone is fearful, but let's consider why anger would show up when someone feels humiliation, rejection, embarrassment, shame, hurt, or some other negative emotion. Fear is in each of these emotions. When we experience one of these negative emotions, we may feel defensive. We defend ourselves when we feel threatened or helpless or lacking control. Anger brings power to these situations too.

> The hormonal arousal from anger can last many hours and even days, leaving us vulnerable to ongoing irritation and new angry episodes. In addition, **anger brings secondary gain.** It helps release pent-up stress, acts as a shield by covering up painful emotions (i.e. fear, loss, guilt, shame), gets attention, pushes people to act and feels righteous. Though it's tough to disengage it, indulging in

doi.org/10.1016/j.physbeh.2007.05.057.

28 "Neuroscientifically Challenged," @neurochallenged, accessed June 22, 2022, https://neuroscientificallychallenged.com/.

anger leads to more anger, leaves others defensive and distant, and sets up possible harm—emotional, physical or both, creating a cycle of defensiveness and resentment that's hard to break.[29]

Let's look at Jennifer's anger. Before the anger stunt double was called in, the primary feeling she felt was probably hurt or humiliation. *I must not be important to Daun. She forgot about me.* Maybe it is embarrassment. *I went in and sat at a table for two alone and looked foolish.* Maybe fear. *Daun doesn't like me anymore.*

Anger comes because we don't deal with the primary feelings. Some people can't. It is much harder for men to do this if they have been raised (as they often are) to believe that these primary painful emotions make them weak or vulnerable. I teach people that if they deal with the primary feelings, the anger doesn't come. *You can do your own stunts.* Chris Evans, who plays Captain America, does many of his own stunts. Here is one of my real life examples, and believe me, I have a library of personal examples!

When my grandson was born, his mother, Amber, did not care much for me. Her mother came to visit from Kentucky, and I could tell I was the odd woman out. The day after Matthew (the cutest baby in the world) was born, I was trying to call Amber to set up a visit on my way to my office. She didn't answer. I called her mom. She didn't answer. I jumped in the shower to go to work and by the time I got out I was pretty

29 Matthew McKay and Peter D. Rogers, *The Anger Control Workbook* (S.l.: Read How You Want, 2008).

angry. My husband was in the kitchen and when he spoke to me, I snapped at him in response. I was very irritated. Then I asked myself this: *What am I afraid of?* I realized that I had skipped over the primary emotion. I acknowledged that I was afraid I would not get to be part of my grandson's life. Once I identified the primary feelings and the fear they generated, there was no more anger. I didn't need a stunt double. I didn't need the power of anger. I acknowledged and dealt with my fear instead.

If you can identify the primary feeling, it is easier to take short account. The easiest way to identify that feeling is to ask yourself what you are afraid of. Ephesians 4:26–27 says, "Be angry, and yet do not sin; do not let the sun go down on your anger, and do not give the devil an opportunity."

Now back to the offense. What are you afraid of? Did the situation cause you to feel hurt? Humiliated? Embarrassed? Afraid? Afraid of what exactly? Were you disappointed or made to feel incapable or unworthy? Did you feel a lack of respect? These feelings are often covered by anger.

Anger has no purpose if you allow yourself to experience those primary negative emotions.

When you can identify the feeling (or state) and allow yourself to experience the feelings that make you feel vulnerable, there is simply no need for anger. It melts away. Anger has no purpose if you allow yourself to experience those primary negative emotions.

Sometimes when people struggle to feel negative emotions, I let them know they are in the very best of company. Jesus experienced all of it: pain, hurt, humiliation, betrayal, and fear. Acknowledging and understanding that our Lord experienced these painful emotions sometimes helps people experience them too, without getting defensive and angry. Defensiveness always comes from pride and pride is a way to protect ourselves.

Righteous Indignation

According to *Webster's Unabridged Dictionary*, *indignation* means "anger mingled with contempt, disgust."[30] I could have referred to this as "Righteous Anger" but we already stated that emotions are not bad or good; they are indicators of our beliefs. Therefore, it is important to say a few words about righteous indignation because it is my experience that when discussing anger in any form, the question will come up: "Well, what about *righteous* anger?"

I have spent my life advocating for people: people with mental health issues, people with developmental disabilities, and people who live in poverty. These vulnerable populations don't always have a voice and sometimes experience exploitation. For several years, I was an education advocate and attended local Committees of Special Education meetings on behalf of students with disabilities and their families to make sure the students' rights to a free and appropriate education were not being violated.

---

30 "Indignation Definition & Meaning," *Webster's Unabridged Dictionary*, part of the public domain at Project Gutenberg.

I was working with a student who had severe social anxiety. She was being tutored at home because she could not function in school. I do not usually advocate home tutoring for anxiety because avoidance is the primary coping strategy for anxiety. However, the circumstances surrounding this student's condition were exceptional, so she received home tutoring while we diligently worked to integrate her back into school.

A helpful aspect in all this was that she loved playing basketball and was comfortable playing in school because her best friend was on the team. She was excited to join basketball. Her mother called the school, and the principal let her know that if she was not in school, she could not play. She was very upset, and so was her daughter when she found out.

I was angry too. I was experiencing righteous indignation. My anger was an indicator of my recognition of the injustice that had occurred. It was wrong to punish someone for their disability. The laws clearly supported Stephanie playing basketball, even though she was being tutored at home.

Righteous indignation has spurred some of the greatest activism and positive social change in history. Jesus certainly experienced some righteous indignation when He walked up the stairs of the synagogue and declared it a den of thieves, overturning the tables of the money changers tables in Matthew 21:12. But the anger associated with this event could have easily motivated negative or adversarial behavior or change. We cannot lose sight of the outcome we want to achieve. Jesus' outcome was to declare the synagogue holy and remove the people that were desecrating the temple. He did not get carried away with His anger and harm the wrongdoers. Jesus' goal was to restore the temple worship, which He did.

I once worked with the family of a student with a learning disability in a very small community. The student was not permitted to go on a field trip because his aide was not available to go. This mother could have easily advocated on behalf of her child, so he could have gone on the trip. Instead, she let her indignation lead her down a path of slander, lies, and manipulation. The anger was an indicator in this case, again, of an injustice. However, the behavior that resulted did not achieve the desired outcome. The student missed the field trip and the mother's behavior discredited her, and made her less effective as an advocate for her son later on with the school.

Righteous indignation occurs when we become upset by injustice or cruelty. When you experience this, ask yourself, *What is the outcome I want to achieve?* Use this energy to create positive change and growth. Be a world changer.

PRINCIPLE 10:
PURPOSEFUL FEAR

> Those who live in the shelter of
> the Most High will find rest in the
> shadow of the Almighty.
> (Psalm 91:1)

I referred to this principle as "purposeful fear" because fear is important and can save our lives. The purpose of the fear response that originates in the amygdala helps us in the presence of danger. According to 2 Timothy 1:7 (NKJV), "God has not given us a spirit of fear, but of power and of love and of a sound mind." In some versions, the word *timidity* is used for *fear*. So, how can fear be purposeful and God-given if Paul told us God did not give us a spirit of fear?

I am writing this during the COVID-19 "stay in place" order. As a counselor and minister, people are coming to me, and they are afraid. They are afraid of losing their jobs, getting sick, or losing vulnerable people to COVID-19. I often hear Christians quoting the verse above, and I hear people who are afraid condemn themselves for being afraid. They feel ashamed and guilty because of their fear.

Let's look at that verse in its context. This was in Paul's second letter to Timothy, Paul's companion and disciple. This letter was written by Paul while he was in prison. At the time, Paul likely knew that he was going to be put to death soon and would never see his dear friend, who was like a son to him, again. He was encouraging, admonishing, and instructing.

Scripture tells us that Timothy was timid. I suspect he had a gentle character. If we read more of what Paul wrote to him in 2 Timothy, it reads thus:

> God has not given us a spirit of fear but of power and of love and of a sound mind. So do not be ashamed of the testimony of our Lord, nor of me, his prisoner, but share with me in the sufferings for the gospel according to the power of God. (2 Timothy 1:7–8)

Paul was encouraging Timothy to speak the truth of the gospel with boldness and to be an advocate for the kingdom. He wanted Timothy to boldly declare the Word of God. This brings us back to the question: What does the verse "God has not given us a spirit of fear" mean? The word for *fear* in this passage in Greek is *deilia* meaning "cowardice or timidity."[31]

It reminds me of this: Several years ago I went on a mission trip to the New York School of Urban Ministry (NYSUM). Our group was doing a lot of street ministry and I was praying

---

31 James Strong, "G1167 - Deilia - Strong's Greek Lexicon (KJV)," Blue Letter Bible, accessed June 22, 2022, https://www.blueletterbible.org/lexicon/g1167/kjv/tr/0–1/.

with some women who only spoke Spanish. I was afraid that I would not be received well and would not do a good job because I had difficulty with the language barrier. I felt very timid and out of my element. I pushed through it, but I felt like Timothy may have felt. He too may have shied away from ministry opportunities as a result. Paul was encouraging Timothy to minister in spite of feeling this way. I might also add that in Philippians 2:20, Paul said this about Timothy: "I have no one else like him, who will show genuine concern for your welfare" (NIV). Obviously, if Timothy had lived a life paralyzed by fear, Paul would not have considered him capable to carry out the ministry he had charged him with.

Back to COVID-19. People are afraid. Let's examine this fear and understand that fear serves a purpose. We know that the amygdala is responsible for emotions in the part of the brain **Anxiety is always dread of the future.** that triggers fear. The amygdala typically begins a fear response before we are conscious of the thing we are afraid of. Fear is always for right now. This is very important to understand as we often use the words *fear* and *anxiety* interchangeably.

Anxiety is always dread of the future. Sometimes that future could be an event occurring the following day. When we all heard the initial news about COVID-19 and how it had made its way to the United States, we experienced great fear. This was a normal response to a situation that we had never experienced in our collective lifetime before. As a result, people began following the news regarding COVID-19 and making preparations. I am only referring to fear, not the anxiety that came with it. Planning for the future is necessary. When we just have dread for what the future brings, we get sick.

A fear response will help us to appropriately act in a situation. As a result of this response, we may avoid harm or even death. The fear response that God created us with is supposed to keep us safe. Our beliefs can sometimes cause us to fear people, places, and things that are not harmful, or to expect danger where there is none. Sometimes we are taught to fear things based on someone else's perceived sense of danger. In any case, feeling fearful is based on our belief of what constitutes danger. The problem is that sometimes we believe lies. Let's look at the difference perspective makes.

PRINCIPLE 11:
THE FEAR AND FAITH CONNECTION

What I always feared has
happened to me. What I dreaded
has come true.
(Job 3:25)

Now faith is the certainty of
things hoped for, a proof of things
not seen.
(Hebrews 11:1 NASB)

Now that we have talked about fear and its intended purpose, let's talk about fear that may be a response to things that are not necessarily dangerous. Anxiety, worry, and fear are alive and well in our society. Instead of fostering resiliency, we sometimes coddle, excuse, and justify. Our young adults and children are under great pressure to perform. This, coupled with social media and increasing, unrealistic demands on our children, is affecting their interpersonal skills. Don't get me wrong; people are broken and hurting and need love. However, too often people are willing to address conflict on social media, but are ill-equipped and unwilling to properly address it in their real life interactions. Bullying is commonplace. I am seeing a significant number of students of all ages laden with anxiety. Some have anxiety so severe that they cannot attend school.

When someone comes to my practice with anxiety, I look at many factors. Some of these include psychosomatization or the physical manifestations of the anxiety; trauma or the root of the anxiety, if recoverable; and the physical, chemical, developmental, and neurological processes that can affect this, such as, did the person just start menstruating? Obviously we explore interpersonal, psychological, and emotional responses and processes.

I worked with a fourteen-year-old girl named June. She came to me with significant anxiety about spending the night at people's houses because she was afraid she would vomit at her friends' houses and be embarrassed and ruin the evening. Upon examination, it turned out that June had spent the night at her aunt's with whom she had a close relationship. She frequently slept over with her aunt and cousin. She shared that the last time she spent the night there, she became sick and had to go home. According to her mom, she got a stomach bug. What June remembered and paired is that she got sick and threw up while spending the night at her aunt's house and ruined the evening. Her mom had to come and take her home. Her cousin was sad that they couldn't hang out.

One of the first things we did was to visually create a toolbox. We were going to put tools in the box, so that she felt equipped to deal with these situations. We discussed that our goal was to eradicate the fear of sleeping at friends' houses.

Additionally, I suggested to her mother that she check in with her doctor, get some bloodwork done, and check things out physically. Her pediatrician did refer her to a gastroenterologist. Thirty years ago, our first line of defense was to rule out anything physical, and I believe strongly in this. We are a triune being: body, mind, and spirit. The body and mind seek to be in alignment, ideally with the spirit. Things that affect our body can easily affect our mind and vice versa. Hyperthyroidism, for example, can cause anxiety. Diabetes can cause attention deficit. So it is important to rule out physical factors.

We had an empty toolbox to fill and had ruled out physical causes. I let June know that she had a gift of faith. She looked at me, confused. "What? How?" she asked. She couldn't see a connection.

We looked at her symptoms. A couple of weeks following the first incident at her aunt's house, she made arrangements to spend the night at her friend Alissa's house. She stated that three hours before leaving her stomach got upset. She began to worry that she would throw up, and canceled the overnight stay out of fear.

This happened over and over. She couldn't even stay at her aunt's house after a while. June enjoyed sleepovers. She was very social and these symptoms devastated her. Additionally, the anxiety was growing. I often refer to anxiety as "mind cancer." When left untreated, anxiety often morphs and grows into other areas, creating devastating strongholds. What's more, the primary coping mechanism for anxiety is avoidance. This only fortifies its strongholds.

Think about it this way. I am afraid of spiders. My husband says I need professional help for this each time I screech for him to come and kill a spider. Because I am afraid of spiders, I avoid them. In the summer, I keep my windows up on my car and I stay out of my basement. The problem with avoidance is that it enhances anxiety. Our minds are very powerful. My avoidance allows my mind to now further define the problem. This means that my fear and anxiety have fertile ground in the garden of my active imagination!

It is this same principle about our powerful minds that showed me that June had a gift of faith. When I first became a Christian, I was taught that fear was the opposite of faith. This is simply not true. *Fear is faith in the wrong thing.* If I were to say that I feared I had cancer or some dreadful disease, I could also say it this way: *I have faith I have cancer.* June's faith was so strong that it was manifesting itself in physical ways. She was getting nauseated, having headaches, and vomiting because of the anxiety caused by the pairing of her stomach bug symptoms and the impact it had on her overnight stay with her aunt and cousin. Not only was her faith manifesting in physical ways, it was negatively impacting the people around her too.

> **When we can reframe the mind as being powerful, and present evidence of its power, it diminishes the feeling of being a victim to fear and anxiety.**

When we can reframe the mind as being powerful, and present evidence of its power, it diminishes the feeling of being a victim to fear and anxiety. Evidence is very important. In this case, it meant understanding that fear is faith in the wrong thing. Because June could physically manifest her faith that she would throw up anywhere she spent the night, we discussed the potential for a positive manifestation of her faith in God instead.

We then started the process of normalizing her fear to take the power away from it. We added some over-the-counter nausea medicine and ginger ale to the tool kit along with some snacks June considered "tummy friendly." We also created a narrative she could use with friends and family when she spent the night and self-talk such as: *My stomach is upset, but I can still stay. I will just be careful what I eat when I am there.* She also sat down with her aunt and cousin and discussed the situation. She let them know she might get sick, but wanted to work toward spending the night. Her aunt and cousin were very supportive. They let her know that if she got sick, she could still stay. After about five weeks, she was staying the night at her aunt's again. Two weeks after that, she was staying with friends again. Three weeks more and she felt ready to be discharged from counseling.

This does not work with all situations involving fear and anxiety. It is, however, a great tool for some situations, and in all situations, it's empowering to the individual. Fear and anxiety can be paralyzing. Knowing that you have power in these situations can greatly affect the outcome as well as diminish symptoms or make them more manageable. According to

Philippians 4:6, we should "not be anxious about anything, but in every situation, by prayer and petition, with thanksgiving, present your requests to God" (NIV).

Now let's take a closer look at anxiety and panic. Just as I consider fear as faith in the wrong thing, I often consider panic attacks as misguided fear responses.

PRINCIPLE 12:
ANXIETY AND PANIC

So don't worry about these things,
saying, "What will we eat? What
will we drink? What will we
wear?" These things dominate
the thoughts of unbelievers, but
your heavenly Father already
knows all your needs. Seek the
Kingdom of God above all else,
and live righteously, and he will
give you everything you need.
So don't worry about tomorrow,
for tomorrow will bring its own
worries. Today's trouble is enough
for today.
(Matthew 6:31–34)

People often come to counseling saying they had a panic attack. My first order of business is to determine whether they had a panic attack or an anxiety attack. Panic attacks are more severe with multiple symptoms. One of the most significant differences is that panic attacks may have no known triggers, whereas anxiety attacks are a response to fear or worry. According to the DSMV Diagnostic and Statistical Manual, 5th Edition, a panic attack is:

> An abrupt period of intense fear or discomfort accompanied by four or more of the following thirteen systemic symptoms:
>
> - Palpitations, pounding heart, or accelerated heart rate
> - Sweating
> - Trembling or shaking
> - Shortness of breath or feeling of smothering
> - Feelings of choking
> - Chest pain or discomfort
> - Nausea or abdominal distress
> - Feeling dizzy, unsteady, lightheaded, or faint
> - Chills or heat sensations
> - Paresthesia (i.e., numbness or tingling sensations)
> - Derealization (feeling of unreality) or depersonalization (being detached from oneself)
> - Fear of losing control or going crazy
> - Fear of dying[32]

An anxiety attack (based on what my patients typically describe) refers to experiencing severe anxiety, as with a generalized anxiety disorder (GAD). This disorder is characterized by excessive anxiety and worry about a number of events and

32 *Diagnostic and Statistical Manual of Mental Disorders* (5th Ed) (Washington DC: American Psychiatric Association, 2013).

activities. Worrying is difficult to control. Anxiety and worry are associated with at least three of the following six symptoms when they occur for a majority of the time over a period of at least six months: restlessness or feeling keyed-up or on edge, being easily fatigued, difficulty concentrating or having a sense of your mind going blank, irritability, muscle tension, or sleep disturbance.[33]

We will deal with both of these separately because they require different treatment. First, let's talk about panic attacks. I was meeting with Steven, a seventeen-year-old high school student who was having significant anxiety after having moved. He was very upset to be at a new school. He had difficulty making new friends, which surprised him because he had always had a solid group of friends around him as he had grown up with them in elementary school in a small, rural district.

Panic attacks may have no known triggers, whereas anxiety attacks are a response to fear or worry.

A panic attack occurs when the flight-or-fight response is triggered, even though there is no imminent danger. A person may experience the symptoms of a panic attack when there is no threat. What is fight or flight? In an article by Kendra Cherry, fight or flight is described as:

> A response of the sympathetic nervous system to help arouse us in the event of danger. Adrenaline is

33 Ibid.

released and physiological changes occur to prepare us for fight or flight. Someone in this aroused state will experience rapid heartbeat and breathe faster. His blood flow is concentrated to limbs, muscles, and organs that will help him to fight or flee. Blood flow is safely restricted from his head, digestive, and other systems not necessary during the danger.[34]

Steven shared that when he was playing video games or watching TV, his heart suddenly started racing and his chest got tight. Alarmed greatly, he became more and more anxious. He felt like he was going to pass out and didn't want to lose control, which only escalated his fear.

My first response in this case (and any case) is to rule out anything physical. Although it was very likely a panic attack, I always recommend that a person get checked by their primary care physician first. I have had experience with people experiencing symptoms such as these which turned out to be neurological. Unless a patient obviously has a mental health disorder, I always rule out physical causes first.

Jeanne, another high school student who moved to the area and started school in a new city, came to me with an adjustment disorder, which is an obvious mental health need. Another example is those with PTSD or those seeking support for generalized anxiety, which often has a clear trigger. However, I have a primary care physician order bloodwork to

---

34 Kendra Cherry, "The Fight-or-Flight Response Prepares Your Body to Take Action," Verywell Mind (Verywell Mind, June 10, 2022), https://www.verywellmind.com/what-is-the-fight-or-flight-response-2795194.

rule out thyroid issues and any other possible causes or deficiencies that could be present.

Now back to Steven. We identified his episodes as panic attacks. Typically, I seek to neutralize the problem. This does not mean that I normalize the episode. It means that I calmly present evidence to remove some of the fear which exacerbates and prolongs the episodes. Simple and straightforward information is often a great neutralizer of symptoms. In Steven's case, I pointed out that he didn't need to worry about passing out. I explained that when he had a panic attack, his blood pressure went up, and to pass out, his blood pressure had to go down. These facts helped. Although they didn't eliminate the panic attack, he was able to feel more level-headed, which minimized its effects, once he knew he wasn't going to lose control and pass out. Truth mitigated his fear and helped him remain calmer.

I often recommend exercise for my patients. Doing jumping jacks, running in place (or outside), and other forms of physical exercise help discharge the energy that comes with increased adrenaline. Adrenaline helps in real fight-or-flight situations, but if someone is simply sitting around and playing video games, there is no way to discharge that energy. Running or jumping (I prefer jumping jacks) and any full-body exercise is a great defense. Think about it. If your fight-or-flight response would help you escape a hungry bear, that adrenaline would be very helpful to aid you in running like crazy to safety. Exercise also helps you recognize that you are not having a heart attack. There are many coping mechanisms that help mitigate this.

A splash of cold water to the face helps. Sometimes a cold shower. Healthy self-talk is vital. After you do a few jumping jacks, you can say, "See? It is just a panic attack. My heart is fine. I did not lose control."

I always ask people having panic attacks to log the attack. I am not seeking a lengthy discourse, but checking to see if there is a pattern. I usually request date, time, and a blurb about what was going on prior to its onset. Here are two helpful examples: Twenty-six-year-old Katrina was a married woman without children who worked two jobs, and was referred to me with symptoms of panic attacks. One job was in a local grocery store. After physical issues were ruled out, I asked her to begin journaling.

When we first met, Katrina showed signs of mild anxiety. She felt she was not living up to her potential. She had just completed her master's degree, but was working two jobs to supplement her husband's income. She weighed 226 pounds and told me she was not happy with the way she looked. She experienced panic attacks about three times a week, and had gone to the ER twice. It was the ER doctor that had suggested counseling.

Her journal indicated that typically the panic attack came minutes after she quickly ate during a short break. She would gulp down her food, jump up, begin working again, and one would come. She experienced panic attacks at other times too, but there was a clear pattern emerging. We began normalizing and equipping her with the tools. *Normalizing* is a term I use to describe the process that helps someone feel that their thoughts or behaviors are typical. This takes away some of the fear associated with those thoughts. Doing this is extremely helpful for people to be able to sort them out and deal with them in a healthy manner. Katrina and I discussed the possibility that her panic attacks might be related to her habit of eating so quickly and jumping up to return to work. This plausible idea helped Katrina feel empowered. At her request, we also explored ideas about exercise and weight loss too.

The moment Katrina was armed with truth and tangible activities to combat her anxiety, things changed quickly. She opted for walking instead of jumping jacks and found that walking was a great stress release. She also changed her diet so she was not eating large, carb and fat heavy meals on that short break. She began spacing out her eating and opted for smaller and healthier meals. She enjoyed walking so much, she even walked around in the waiting room before her appointments. She noticed that the attacks became less frequent and less severe. Most important of all, she was no longer afraid of the attacks, and believed they were related to her diet and digestion.

Because of her dietary changes and walking, she began losing weight. After six months, she was discharged from counseling. Later, she started running and working out and lost quite a bit more weight. She looked and felt great and began running 5Ks. Her confidence grew and she pursued a job related to her degree, and eventually moved out of the area to pursue her new career.

This is not going to be everybody's story, but this story changed when Katrina had tangible tools to address the attacks. To begin with, we talked about how fear was a good thing and how it helped in the face of a threat. However,

Katrina's fear was paralyzing and had reduced her quality of life as well as that of her husband. Once the perceived threat was no longer threatening, she was able to move forward with coaching and encouragement. Truth took away the power of the perceived threat.

The other example is that of a twenty-six-year-old married (and pregnant) woman named Tammy with children. Her husband worked long hours and she sometimes experienced symptoms of panic attacks during the evening after dinner. Once again, journaling revealed a pattern. After her blood-work came back normal, we began exploring each episode in detail. Tammy had two young children at home and was seven months pregnant. Her symptoms began prior to her pregnancy, but became more frequent during it. She was very fearful that she was having a heart attack, and was trying very hard to hide her anxiety from her children.

By evening, Tammy's neck and back were sore and she was quite fatigued. I referred her to a chiropractor. I too had experienced back and neck issues that caused tightness in my chest and triggered fear that led to an anxiety attack or mimicked symptoms like a panic attack, so going to a chiropractor was a sensible option.

She shared that the chiropractic care was very helpful and her anxiety symptoms began to subside. We then began tackling the anxiety and stress which was building in her neck and shoulders and contributing to the problem. She was struggling with the demands placed on her, and often felt like a single parent because of the long hours her husband worked. We looked at her natural supports and had a few meetings with

Will, her husband. Meetings with both Tammy and Will allowed us to put in place some prevention planning, with Will as Tammy's helpmate in symptom management. We created particular scripts for Tammy to share with Will when she was experiencing symptoms relating to her anxiety. The scripts were particular statements she could say to Will to let him know she was feeling anxious or fearful. This facilitated open communication between the couple. The scripts did not relieve the stress she felt in running their household on her own while Will worked, but the statements helped Will to *be* supportive and helped Tammy to *feel* supported.

The chiropractic care and intervention plan were tangible tools that relieved some of her stress and helped give her power and control over the perceived threat. This young mama is now doing great and has been out of counseling for seven years.

Let's get back to Steven. Steven continued to experience panic attacks. He did well in implementing interventions when he was having panic attacks and experienced brevity and relief. His journey took much longer, and he left counseling when he could manage symptoms and briefly returned when symptoms became unmanageable.

Both Katrina and Tammy sought to eradicate the anxiety and effects it had on them. They worked hard and made changes. Steven's treatment lasted longer and was less effective because he avoided and did not deal with the source of his anxiety. Avoidance behaviors often make anxiety stronger because anxiety can grow in your mind. Anxiety prevents truth from helping someone have power and control over what they fear.

Not everyone is ready to confront the things in their lives that may contribute to their anxiety. Some people are not able to do this. This is particularly true for people who have experienced trauma. This is a process, and that process is unique to each individual's journey.

Next, let's look at vicarious anxiety. This is anxiety that happens from being around people with anxiety. I see it in many relationships.

PRINCIPLE 13:
VICARIOUS ANXIETY

Don't be afraid, for I am with you.
Don't be discouraged, for I am
your God. I will strengthen you
and help you. I will hold you up
with my victorious right hand.
(Isaiah 41:10)

It is a fact that our character is influenced and affected by the people with whom we spend our time. Motivational speaker Jim Rohn says that we are the average of the five people with whom we spend the most time. I see this often in counseling, particularly with anxiety. Please note that this concept holds true in many other aspects, but I predominantly see people with anxiety or similar disorders.

Samantha was a college student who was in a two-year relationship with Stephan. She began counseling for generalized anxiety. She was struggling with her school work, having memory issues, and experiencing anxiety symptoms regularly. She stated that she constantly felt like she could not meet other people's expectations and feared that she was too needy and imposing. Samantha had no significant history with anxiety, although she shared that she had been a "bit of a worrier" when she was a teenager.

She stated that Stephan was being treated for anxiety for the past several months and was taking a daily dose of Zoloft to help manage his symptoms. About a month and a half into counseling Samantha, Stephan dropped out of school and moved back home to Long Island, about four hours away from SUNY Oswego where they both attended school. Although she clearly grieved the loss of this significant relationship in her life, within two weeks there was marked improvement in her symptoms. About six weeks into counseling, she was experiencing no anxiety and discontinued counseling. We used this time to discuss how Stephan's anxiety had impacted her and how vicarious anxiety led to these destructive symptoms. The final few weeks of counseling before discharge was psychoeducation and prevention.

Psychology and biology are a typical lens through which we view anxiety, but social learning theory lends credence to vicarious anxiety. Albert Bandura is a psychologist and founder of social learning theory. According to social learning theory, thoughts and behavior can be learned through observing how other people think and behave. In other words, we learn through other people's experience in addition to our own.[35] Although I may sound like Captain Obvious for pointing this out, the truth is that we don't always understand anxiety as being a learned process through observation. *Social experiences are critical in the development of anxiety disorders.*

35 Albert Bandura, *Social Learning Theory* (Englewood Cliffs, N.J: Prentice-Hall, 1977).

Often we don't even realize the impact our behavior has on the people around us. This is especially true for our children. Parent after parent will share how they don't want their anxiety or panic to impact their children, so they leave the room to make sure they are not around them. Yet their children develop symptoms anyway. Although some of this may be hereditary, much is learned through observation. Well-meaning parents try hard not to appear anxious around their children, but it is not only the overt symptoms that children pick up on. Children are tuned in to the subtle nuances as well.

Often we don't even realize the impact our behavior has on the people around us.

I stated previously that I am afraid of spiders when I was discussing avoidance as a coping strategy. I have three boys, and when my oldest son Danny was 20, he and I went on a road trip to a rock concert in Columbus, Ohio. Following the concert, we went to Lorain to stay with family. I found myself on a country road around 11:30 pm when the unthinkable happened. A spider ran across my windshield, and as I passed under one of the few streetlamps on the road, I could tell he was on the inside. I immediately pulled over, jumped out of the car, and screamed, "Kill it!" at my son, who was still in the car. He looked bewildered, so I informed him (in one long yell) that there was a spider on the windshield. KILL IT! What happened next surprised me. I expected him to find and smash it with his hand, so I could be comforted by the remains of the spider on the windshield. Instead, he jumped out of the car—just as afraid as I was. I never knew he was afraid of spiders.

We yelled back and forth over the roof of the car about who was going to kill the spider. By the time we got back in the car, we couldn't find the spider. This story became one of the many great dinner narratives our family has!

The only negative experience Danny had ever had with spiders up to that point was his awareness that I was afraid of them. Later, he had his own personal "spider experience" which occurred only after he learned to be afraid of spiders through observing me. Not only did this lend credence to his observation, but it also determined his response to the stimuli (the spider).

Social learning theory helps us understand how anxiety disorders develop through our social experiences. Albert Bandura states that "learning would be extremely laborious, not to mention hazardous, if people had to rely solely on their own actions to inform them what to do." According to social learning theory, people not only learn through their direct experiences, but also vicariously through observing others' experiences.[36] This is fundamental in understanding vicarious anxiety and the development of some anxiety disorders as is illustrated in the relationship between Samantha and Stephan or the example of my son Daniel with spiders. Social learning theory also explains why different people respond differently to anxiety-producing thoughts or situations.

Understanding social learning theory gives us more tools to deal with anxiety and other problems. Sometimes when people understand that the root of their anxiety or fear was gained

---

36 Ibid.

through observing and assimilating someone else's responses, it takes away some of its power.

We should also be aware in our relationships that we are not giving or receiving an impartation of anxiety or fear. Remember, the feelings we have are real and true, but the beliefs may be the problem. We must be thoughtful and diligent that we are not imparting wrong beliefs on the people around us and "take every thought captive to the obedience of Christ" (2 Cor. 10:5) over every belief others may impart to us. These are responsibilities that we each have. In our humanity, we may not do it perfectly, but we should never stop persevering.

When we let fear and anxiety make our decisions, we are giving whatever (or whoever) is causing the fear and anxiety power over us. Let's further examine some of the possible outcomes of fear and anxiety.

PRINCIPLE 14:
STAY OUT OF YOUR HEAD!

Finally, brothers, whatever is true,
whatever is honorable, whatever is
just, whatever is pure, whatever is
lovely, whatever is commendable,
if there is any excellence, if there
is anything worthy of praise, think
about these things. What you
have learned and received and
heard and seen in me—practice
these things, and the God of
peace will be with you.
(Philippians 4:8–9 ESV)

Spending too much time being introspective and getting to know oneself can lead to negativity, depression, anxiety, and self-sabotage. Self-sabotage undermines a person's success despite their wishes and dreams. This happens with excessive introspection. An individual can easily make the shift to focusing on problems and not solutions. You might ask, *What if I can spend all day sitting and thinking about myself and my circumstances and remain positive through all of my sitting and thinking?*

I work hard not to say *always* or *never* unless I really mean always or never. Yes, there is a possibility that you will spend a whole day sitting and thinking about you and your circumstances, and still successfully challenge yourself to remain positive throughout the exercise. I have two questions: (1) How easy was this for you if you were not diligently conscious about the process? and (2) How did spending a whole day sitting and thinking about yourself enrich you and the world around you?

Introspection allows you to really get to know yourself on a deep level and gives you understanding and insight into your behaviors and thoughts, right? It helps you create your best version of *you*, right? Unfortunately, the answer to both those questions is no, not really. Humans are not meant to be alone, sitting around, in their heads and thinking about themselves. God created us to be interactive, and in fellowship and relationship. The best

> **God created us to be interactive, and in fellowship and relationship.**

way to heal from hurt, disappointment, sadness, and emotional pain is by pouring into others and letting God take care of you. Imagine the world if we all did that!

Now, don't get me wrong. I am not in any way saying that being introspective in a moderate, healthy way is bad. Indeed, it is biblical. We are encouraged to practice solitude in the context of belonging to the family of God. It is important for us to self-evaluate. In 2 Corinthians 13:5, Paul tells us to examine ourselves. In Romans 12:3, we are told to think of ourselves with sober judgment. What would be an example of this?

Justine was talking to her friend, Tabitha. The two were discussing a colleague at work, and Tabitha shared that she thought a guy named Michael was interested in dating her. Justine facetiously remarked, "Well, that's interesting." Tabitha abruptly moved on to another topic.

After the interaction, Justine replayed the interaction in her mind. Through her introspection, she realized that she may have offended Tabitha or at the very least, made her uncomfortable with her remark. The next day at work, Justine approached Tabitha and apologized for her words.

This was purposeful introspection and love in action. When Justine evaluated the situation, she realized she may have hurt Tabitha and came to the conclusion that she needed to apologize. The next day she sought her out. Her self-evaluation also gave her conviction. This was also purposeful. Negative emotions can help to evaluate ourselves.

Here is another example. Johnny was thirty-two years old, single, and by his own account, miserable. He did delivery work for a living, and had plenty of time to spend in his car, thinking about his situation. He wanted to lose weight and when he had eaten poorly for a day, he would often spend a couple of hours thinking about his failure. Since he was such a failure in his mind, he sometimes stopped at a convenience store and bought snack cakes and Slim Jims. He continued to think about himself and felt angry at this new failure, which seemed to further prove the "truth" of his viewpoint. He felt he could not change, so why bother? When friends called him on the road, he would sound sad and depressed and tell them what a failure he was. This initially resulted in them trying to

encourage and support him, but eventually they stopped calling because they did not wish to be negatively impacted by his
repeated depressing statements about himself.

Why did this happen? Simple. The word *encourage* is a
verb. According to Oxford Languages it means to "give support, confidence or hope to someone." *It implies action.* It is
about giving. All behavior is intentional. There is no such thing
as accidental behavior. When a friend to Johnny was giving
him support and trying to lift him up, that was an intentional
act. When the purpose of someone's behavior is not realized,
the behavior stops. When Johnny kept needing the encouragement but was not changing his words and thoughts, the
encouragement from others lost its purpose. Instead of being
encouraged, Johnny's words and behaviors discouraged the
friends that were trying to help. This was not the purpose of
their encouragement, so they stopped giving it.

Meanwhile, Johnny just got more depressed and angry
at his friends for "letting him down." His behavior became
self-sabotaging. Depending on where he was in this cycle, he
acted in two different ways. His one behavior was an "I'll show
them" attitude (due to his bitterness and unforgiveness toward
them) for no longer giving him the verbal encouragement they
used to provide. He would return to a good diet, lose a few
pounds, and do well for a short time. Eventually though, he
would fall back into his poor eating habits and begin that cycle
again. His other choice would be to not bother with any of that
and simply blame his friends for his situation, continue eating
poorly, and put on even more weight. These behavior patterns
continued until he'd hit bottom and begin again, often losing

friends along the way. This is a common pattern with any entitlement complex.

So the reason people don't usually sit around and think positive thoughts about themselves and their circumstances is because *positive thinkers are doers*. People who are positive aren't just thinking about themselves and their problems. They are doing. They are engaging. They are sharing. They are relating. (They are also grateful people.)

Johnny wasn't "doing." He mistakenly framed "doing" as the verbal encouragement he received from well-meaning friends. If encouragement was an actor, it would be in a supportive role. It would not be the main character who fueled the story and kept it moving. The encouragement itself is a catalyst; it is not the event.

Positive thinkers are doers.

A catalyst produces a reaction or precipitates an event. The responsibility for his choice to act or do nothing falls on Johnny. He could always have chosen to *act* upon the encouragement and support he received. The action he took would have engendered gratitude in his heart toward his friends and help him grow in humility at the same time, as it overcame the unhealthy behavioral cycles in his life.

Was it wrong for Johnny to be thoughtful about his failure? Absolutely not! It was necessary and helpful. He just needed to engage in it in a different way. Johnny ate poorly and spent a lot of time focused on his failure. This convinced him that he was a failure. Let's put Johnny's thought process in a different framework.

If you were to go to the doctor with a headache, severe pain and swelling in your face, and a stuffy nose, your doctor would diagnose you with a sinus infection. The diagnosis is negative news. Is it necessary? Yes, it is. Is it serving a purpose? Yes. A diagnosis is necessary for treatment to occur. Once you diagnose a problem, you can formulate its solution. The doctor will send you home with a recommended treatment that could include a prescription for antibiotics and nasal rinse. She might want to see you again for a follow-up appointment in a week. You are expected to follow the treatment prescribed so you can get better. You don't go home and live in the problem. You don't sit around and dwell on the fact that you are sick with a sinus infection. Let's pretend that Johnny had a sinus infection instead of a diet problem, but treated it the same way as he did cheating on his diet.

- Johnny felt awful, went to the doctor and was diagnosed with a sinus infection. The doctor gave him a prescription for penicillin and instructed him to use a nasal rinse. He also set up a follow-up appointment.
- Johnny was discouraged. He went home and thought about his diagnosis all day. He felt like a failure because he had this infection. How did he let it get so bad? He was practically incapacitated. He knew he should rest, but instead he felt that he really needed to understand how this sinus infection had occurred in his life.
- He told his friends he had a sinus infection. His friends encouraged him and supported him. "Make sure you take your antibiotics," they said. One of his friends offered to

pick up his medicine and bring it to him, but Johnny said he'd take care of that himself and continued to be distressed by his situation. Johnny thought: *I wonder who gave me this sinus infection?* He decided to focus on how sick he was and how he felt. He became more and more depressed, but also a little angry, but that was only because he was too tired and sick to be really angry. He used what little energy he had left to dwell on his sickness.

• Meanwhile, he never went to the pharmacy for his medicine, never took it, and just felt worse and worse as his body tried to fight it off without any help.

We are not meant to dwell on our diagnosis; we are meant to dwell on our healing. We are not meant to dwell on the problem; we are meant to dwell on the solution. The purpose of a diagnosis is for identification. We need to identify the problem so we know how to treat it, so we can create a plan for healing. Once a diagnosis is given, there is no purpose in dwelling on it. Once a treatment plan has been found, the purpose for the diagnosis has been fulfilled.

Using the example of Johnny having a sinus infection as a parallel to his diet failure probably seemed preposterous, but it is an accurate illustration of what happens when we dwell on problems and not solutions. We become paralyzed. It is easy to sit around and dwell on our problems. We need to take responsibility for our problems. That requires that we take initiative as we meditate on the solution and come up with a plan. This creates positive action.

Let's revisit the sinus infection scenario to look at how a focus on the solution would change the outcome:

- Johnny gets the diagnosis and a treatment plan is created. Johnny is feeling sick, tired, and depressed, and his friend calls to support him and offers to pick up his antibiotics.
- A very grateful Johnny lets his friend know how helpful that would be. The same friend brings him his medication and suggests that Johnny rests.
- Johnny takes the antibiotic, has a cup of tea, and watches TV before falling asleep.
- The friend that picked up his antibiotic was blessed by Johnny's gratitude and tells another friend that Johnny is sick.
- She brings Johnny homemade chicken noodle soup the next day.
- Johnny continues his treatment and his friends check on him and support him.
- Within three days, Johnny is feeling significantly better and improving speedily.

In this scenario, Johnny focused on the solution and not the problem, and he got better. Johnny wasn't just sitting around and thinking about the solution. He thought about it and then acted upon it. He became a doer. He participated in his treatment. He took responsibility for getting well.

The moral of the story: If you think and speak a problem, even your faith will be focused on that problem; you will have a problem. If you think and speak a solution, you will have faith for a solution; you will have a solution. We will look at how this principle can rob someone of their dreams and purpose.

PRINCIPLE 15:
DON'T SABOTAGE YOUR DREAMS

Lord, when doubts fill my mind,
when my heart is in turmoil,
quiet me and give me renewed
hope and cheer.
(Psalm 94:19 TLB)

I've done it. We've all done it. You start dreaming about something and pretty soon you are sabotaging that dream with a flurry of negativity. That is what happened to Kenny.

Kenny had a brilliant mind and was quite a dreamer, often presenting innovative new ideas. He frequently talked about starting his own business using some of the ideas he had shared with me. One week he would be ready to dive into a new adventure and then the next week he would come in depressed and defeated. When I asked what had happened, he would say that he thought about his idea, but that in the end, he had realized why his great idea would not work. Time and time again this happened.

What started out as a great dream for a potential service website ended up with Kenny determining that he was not capable of doing it. He thought that if he were to try to do it, he would fail. It seemed that when he thought about a venture too long and hard, his thought line went from a dream to a problem statement to the death of the dream. Once the problem statement set in, perceived failure was imminent—because he dwelt on the problem.

The seeds sown were dark and they multiplied. Thinking on one problem led to thoughts about many other potential problems. From first problem to last, most of Kenny's time was spent in generating negative thoughts. How sad this was! In truth, Kenny he had a great idea with true potential for success!

Kenny and I discussed each problem statement and considered solutions. Any solution brought to the table was quickly dismissed by him. This was not a new course of action for Kenny. He frequently came up with great opportunities that he shot down soon after he conceived them. Why? Why was he problem-focused? Because of his fear. Kenny believed lies about himself and his abilities. When he thought excessively and intensely about any business he wanted to start, he would talk himself right out of that good idea.

Initially, Kenny would have an idea. As he began to imagine more about it and daydream about it, he would get consumed by his dream. He felt great when he was thinking about it. However, it wasn't long before the "what ifs" came along. These were statements that were supposed to help Kenny properly assess the viability of his idea. For instance, Kenny might wonder, *What if I need financing for this project? Where's that going to come from? How is my credit? What if I am overestimating the need for this service?*

There was nothing inherently wrong with these thoughts. In fact, they are necessary, but wait … there's more. Let's say Kenny had this great dream—he daydreamed about it for days. He shared it with friends. Eventually the "what ifs" began to permeate the daydream.

Typically, a "what if" statement acts as or precedes a problem statement. Based on the flow of thoughts outlined above, the problem statement is supposed to follow the idea. It's how we figure out how to execute them. Kenny would move into formulating problem statements, but once he began this process, his list of potential problems got very long, to the point of making it feel insurmountable. Kenny dwelled on the problems so much that thinking about the problems began to generate more problems. Therefore, his dreams just died.

Let's try and tie all of this together. Fear caused the death of Kenny's dreams. He reviewed his list and then believed the lie that he could never accomplish it. He would enter into a looping process that could only be revealed when we pinpointed the lies he was believing about himself and his abilities.

On the outside, this is what his process looked like when he had a dream, followed by the usual problem statement (which produced negative thoughts), and eventually led to the death of the dream, but in reality it was a cluster of lies that sounded like this:

1. "I have great ideas, but do not have the confidence to manifest my dreams because I struggle to be effective in my job and barely got through college."
2. "Something is wrong with me."

3. "I never follow through with anything."
4. "I don't know why I can't do anything." (Kenny lacked the faith that he could be successful.)
5. A new dream or idea.
6. The necessary problem statements.
7. The fact that he had problem statements at all acted as justification for the many lies Kenny believed that are outlined above.
8. These were followed by: "Why did I think this time would be different? I don't know why I let myself think about these things. These ideas never go anywhere."
9. Then came the death of the dream.

If we look at Kenny's history, we might be able to determine the root of the lie he believed about himself. Doing so, however, does not always rectify the equation. We were dealing with a core belief that had been with him since he was in elementary school. He thought he was not capable of having success. This undermined his self-confidence at a deep level. So when he has a great idea and began dwelling on it, his fear immediately took over because it was already in the driver's seat in his mind.

Kenny needed action and accountability. The first change Kenny needed to make was to take immediate action when he had an idea. Action could turn the dream into a vision. Visions can live outside of the imagination; dreams cannot. An action can be initiated by creating a vision statement. From that, Kenny could make goals and form a plan or call someone who could help him establish the steps to realizing his vision. All of these are actions. The action Kenny did take was to share his dream over coffee with anyone who would listen, but that didn't *do* anything.

It is important to expect action so we move out of our comfort zone. In Kenny's case, his choice was to avoid any real action, which further perpetuated the lies he believed about his own capability and worth. Kenny was so fearful of failure that he often spent hours upon hours trying to learn how to prevent failure in his projects. Truly the only way to failure-proof anything is simply not to do it, and that was typically the end result of Kenny's efforts.

> **It is important to expect action so we move out of our comfort zone.**

So, how do we step out in faith and take action? According to Hebrews 11:1, "Faith is confidence in what we hope for and assurance about what we do not see" (NIV). This is one of my favorite Scriptures. True faith requires obedience. I live in central New York. We joke that the county of Oswego is known far and wide because it is so often featured on national weather channels because of the ridiculous record snowfalls we get in the winter. The people I work with through our ministry are very low-income. A few of them have cars, but often do not have the money to maintain them properly. I live in a rural county and having one's own vehicle is necessary to get to and from work.

Trevor had a small SUV with bald tires. It was in the middle of February, the time when our weather is usually at its worst. Trevor took his vehicle to a local shop and was told not to drive it anymore with those tires. It was too dangerous!

Trevor had faith in what the mechanic said, so he did not drive his vehicle until he could afford new tires. This was a tremendous hardship for him and his family, but he had faith that it was dangerous to drive his vehicle with the bald tires. True faith requires obedience. If Trevor had not had faith in what the mechanic said, he may have driven his vehicle anyway, risking his safety and the safety of others, and possibly wrecking the vehicle that was necessary for his job. But because he had faith, he was obedient.

It was not easy. He had to make significant plans to get to and from work, and sometimes that meant staying overnight in another town with a friend. His family, already living paycheck-to-paycheck had to find ways to cut back even more, and Trevor took on some odd jobs to make ends meet and pay for the tires. After four weeks, Trevor left the shop with new tires on his SUV. His faith led to obedience, and his obedience led to a choice that kept him and his family safe. Real faith produces action.

Trevor could have made other choices. He could have chosen to "wing it" and drive even though the vehicle was not safe. The other choice would have been to forfeit his job because he had no reliable transportation. He could have felt that either of these choices were the *only* options. Those other choices would have produced negative actions which manifested in different results.

In making the decision he made and creating a plan to get new tires, Trevor did not become a victim of his circumstances. Typically, it is my experience that there are two predominant forces that contribute to being victimized by one's circumstance: pride and learned helplessness. Pride can prevent you from seeking help or asking for favors. One may be uncomfortable letting his supervisor know that he is in this situation, or that same individual may have a hard time seeking support from friends, family, and coworkers. His pride puts him in a position in which he is on his own without help. Learned helplessness happens when a person suffers from persistent failure, trauma, or otherwise feels powerless. We discussed learned helplessness as part of Principle 7.

Learned helplessness and fear of not being successful were the forces that kept Kenny's vision in the dream state. Together, we began unraveling this fear and Kenny started stepping out in faith in spite of it. His confidence grew as he began to see tangible evidence of the business he was dreaming about. Kenny created a vision from the dream. The vision had the power to live outside of Kenny's mind. Even though the lies he believed still preceded his dream, the vision his faith had activated took the form of action. This brought forth evidence that challenged those lies, removing their power. Even if the evidence only takes away some of the power of a lie, the hurdle that needs to be jumped is not as high as it once was. If Kenny keeps jumping the shorter hurdles, he will build up strength and agility to jump the higher ones. In other words, when we exercise the ability to take action in spite of feeling powerless, we erode the power from the lies we believe about ourselves and the world around us.

Today, when Kenny forms his "what if" statements, they lack power to sabotage his great idea, but do what they are supposed to do instead. He is using his imagination to form various potential problems, so he can come up with solutions for them and work around them. Considering problems is a healthy part of formulating a plan. A problem statement is useful, but it needs to be just that: a statement with the purpose of ushering in a solution, not a statement to discourage and kill the dream.

Again, this is no different than going to the doctor and getting a diagnosis for an ailment. You can play out the diagnosis in your imagination to the point of exacerbating sickness in your body, or you can use the diagnosis to make changes, know what to pray for, and help yourself overcome the ailment.

Kenny also sought accountability in his process. Instead of just sharing his dreams with his friends, he started a business and reported about which stage of the development process he was in. He also shared time frames for key features in development, creating accountability to his friends. More accountability occurred when he gave tasks to his wife to complete that were contingent upon the action he was taking. His wife was eager to help him now because she recognized that Kenny was actively working toward something, not just daydreaming about it.

Action and accountability both create tangible evidence in different ways. Action results in a completed business plan or a meeting with the bank. Accountability creates evidence in that it brings people on board to help, edify, correct, and support. When there is no vision or no action leading to vision, the involvement of accountability partners will fade away. This further fed the lies Kenny had in his head: *See, nobody wants to help me. Even* **they** *know I can't do this.* It is important to find people who really want to invest in you.

It is also important to be humble. Pride prevents proper accountability with accountability partners. When you seek accountability, you are making a commitment. If your pride prevents you from being open and vulnerable about where you are in the process, then the accountability process will break down and you will feed on the lies that prevent the growth of the dream. Initially Kenny's pride made it difficult for him to be accountable to anyone. To him, all correction looked like criticism. He met correction with defensiveness and sometimes anger. This understanding of correction further built up the lies he believed about his worth and ability.

Pride prevents proper accountability with accountability partners.

Paul talked about edification throughout his letters. *Edify* means "to instruct and improve especially in moral and religious knowledge."[37] The root of the word comes from the Latin term *aedificationem,* which means "construction or building."[38] Edification is one of my favorite words. It means to build up. You will often find it with words like *encouragement,* but also with the word *correction.* After all, how is one built up without correction? If one could improve without correction, wouldn't

---

37 "Edify Definition & Meaning," *Webster's Unabridged Dictionary,* part of the public domain at Project Gutenberg.

38 Douglas Harper, "Edification (n.)," Etymology, accessed July 5, 2022, https://www.etymonline.com/word/edification.

that imply that there is no correction needed and therefore nothing to improve?

The difference between correction and criticism is in the heart of the giver. Correction done in love will edify. It will build somebody up. It is important for us to always examine our hearts and make sure we are seeking to build people up, not tear them down. Hurting people hurt people. If correction is given from a place of hurt or need for control, it is criticism. Criticism often condemns and is not proceeding from a right heart.

This was the case with Kenny. Kenny's father was critical. Kenny felt he could not meet his father's expectations, and his dad was often condemning. This was especially hard on Kenny because he desperately wanted his father's approval, but continually fell short, even when he was working hard.

As a result, Kenny perceived all correction as critical and condemning. He was easily offended and felt insulted when corrected. He needed to be edified, which helped destroy the power of the lies he believed about himself. This made way for Kenny to feel safe, so he could allow himself to be accountable. *Accountability requires vulnerability.*

Today, Kenny owns a successful business. He still deals with fear, and some of the lies he believes about himself (in the form of core beliefs) are still there, but they no longer have the power to produce failure in his life. What's more is that the power the lies do still have is diminishing over time as he continues to see evidence of his successes. Kenny's beliefs about himself, his worth, and ability continue to grow and change.

A Quick Look at the Importance of Imagination

Imagination is a powerful catalyst in manifesting faith. God gave us imagination. It is easy to understand the power imagination has in manifesting faith when we look at children play. Children imagine a scenario, take what they have developed in their imagination, and play it out as if those make-believe situations are actual reality. Imagination is a useful tool in problem solving, decision making, and being purpose-driven. Imagining offers perspective and insight.

Sometimes we are so concerned with knowledge that we underestimate the power of our imagination. Some think the Bible regards imagining as a negative concept as in 1 Corinthians 8:2: "If anyone imagines that he knows something, he does not yet know as he ought to know" (ESV). However, this verse is really about knowledge, not using one's imagination. There are many references to imagination in the Old Testament. For example, Genesis 6:5: "And God saw that the wickedness of man was great in the earth, and that every imagination of the thoughts of his heart was only evil continually" (KJV). The Hebrew word used here for imagination is *yetser* which means "a form, framing, purpose."[39] In the following paragraph, you could replace the word *imagination* with *intent*.

> Imagination is one of the most glorious aspects of being human. As far as we know, ants and armadillos

---

39 James Strong, "3336. Yetser," Strong's Hebrew: 3336. רֵצֵי (yetser) -- a form, framing, purpose, accessed June 22, 2022, https://biblehub.com/hebrew/3336.htm.

don't have it. The imagination allows us to think of what is not, to build new mental universes, to apprehend barely conceivable truths, to think ourselves into other people's places and circumstances. The imagination doesn't ask our permission as it traverses perceptions and meanings.[40]

Imagination is a powerful tool that not only helps us turn our dreams into visions but also helps us manage negative emotions.

---

40 Kathryn Reklis et al., "Imagination Is at the Heart of Faith," The Christian Century, April 5, 2019, https://www.christiancentury.org/article/editors/imagination-heart-faith.

PRINCIPLE 16:
HOLD ALL THOUGHTS CAPTIVE

For as he thinks in his heart,
so is he.
(Proverbs 23:7 NKJV)

When we get a thought, we get to choose what we do with it. Right now I am thinking thoughts related to writing about this principle. I formulate a thought and then assess what the outcome of that thought should be. Some thoughts I cast out of my head because they do not convey the message I want to share. Others I cultivate like seeds sprinkled with imagination because they allow me to visualize and elaborate on that concept.

We can choose whether or not we wish to cultivate a thought seed into something greater. Like any seed, it first germinates, then a plant grows, and in time, fruit is produced.

> A good tree can't produce bad fruit, and a bad tree can't produce good fruit. A tree is identified by its fruit. Figs are never gathered from thornbushes, and grapes are not picked from bramble bushes. A

good person produces good things from the treasury of a good heart, and an evil person produces evil things from the treasury of an evil heart. What you say flows from what is in your heart. (Luke 6:43–45)

Sometimes we have a seed that would produce good fruit, but we don't cultivate it and it does not have a chance to bear good fruit. Other times we have a seed that produces bad fruit, and we cultivate this seed with great care, bearing the bad fruit.

The "thought seeds" we sow either form or support our core beliefs. Core beliefs are the deeply held assumptions that determine how we see ourselves, the people around us, and our world. "*Core beliefs* are strongly-held, rigid, and inflexible beliefs that are maintained by the tendency to focus on information that supports the belief and ignoring information that contradicts it."[41] It's as if a core belief was a magnet that attracted thoughts that validated and strengthened itself. Over time, we will accept this belief as truth and fact, making it very difficult to change this belief. The belief is so deeply etched in our hearts that we don't even realize how and when it affects

> **The "thought seeds" we sow either form or support our core beliefs.**

---

41 "Factsheet," CCI, accessed June 22, 2022, https://www.cci.health. wa.gov.au/-/media/CCI/Mental-Health-Professionals/Depression/Depression---Information-Sheets/Depression-Information-Sheet---12---What-are-Core-Beliefs.pdf.

our behavior unless we have previously identified it. Common destructive core beliefs are *I am unlovable* or *I'm not good enough*.

In ministry and counseling, I like to refer to core beliefs as heart beliefs. Your mind holds your thoughts; your heart holds your beliefs. This is very simplistic, of course, but it provides an easy-to-use framework. Let's explore the importance of holding your thoughts captive to being obedient to Christ first by studying this verse from a letter Paul wrote to the Corinthian church:

> For the weapons of our warfare are not of the flesh but have divine power to destroy strongholds. We destroy arguments and every lofty opinion raised against the knowledge of God, and take every thought captive to obey Christ. (2 Corinthians 10:4–5 ESV)

Paul is responding to his critics in Corinth. Some had set themselves in opposition to Paul and claimed that even though he talked a good game in his letters, he was pathetic and weak in person. In other words, the opposition was calling Paul a poser. Paul assured them earlier in the letter in 2 Corinthians 1–18 that when he arrived, he and his cohorts were prepared to confront these "false apostles" with boldness in Christ. Paul stated that he would hold the thoughts of the Corinthians (who had been wrongly influenced by these false apostles) captive and affirm their obedience to Christ. He was literally talking about capturing their thoughts for Christ as a response to the false apostles capturing their thoughts. These ideas were in conflict with the teachings of Christ.

So let's take a look at our thoughts. Thoughts come and go swiftly in our minds. A thought is defined as "an idea, a mental conception."[42] I often feel that the sudden thoughts I get during prayer result from communication by the Holy Spirit. Much of the time, however, my mind is filled with a wellspring of ideas and opinions that are being formulated as I go through my day. We all have thoughts. What do we do with them? What are the options?

The idea of holding thoughts captive to the obedience of Christ is simply stating that we need to keep our minds captive to Christ. This is a great responsibility for the believer. Christ, during His ministry, gave us many strategies and was a living example of this. He spent a great deal of time in prayer and only did what the Father told Him to do.

Doers are not as plagued by bad thoughts.

The more I commune with my Father, the easier it is for me to hear His voice and the leadings of the Holy Spirit. You can also evaluate your thoughts by determining if they will harm someone or cause someone to stumble. Will this thought be harmful to you or someone else? It is important to make these evaluations.

As Paul explained in Romans 12:3,: "Think of yourself with sober judgment" (NIV). I review my thoughts and deeds each night so that I may reflect, make correction, make amends if

---

42 "Thought Definition & Meaning," *Webster's Unabridged Dictionary*, part of the public domain at Project Gutenberg.

necessary, learn, and grow. Here are seven strategies I use that may help you to cast out thoughts that keep your mind from being obedient to Christ.

1. The Kingdom Test. A primary strategy, the Kingdom Test has helped many people. I heard this term in an audio sermon several years ago and don't recall who was speaking, but the concept has stuck with me and continues to be helpful to those I counsel. If a thought pops into your head, but you are not entirely sure if it is something you should entertain or not, the Kingdom Test will help. Ask yourself, *Will what I am thinking about advance the kingdom of God?* Answering this question will help you to determine whether or not this is a thought you want to cultivate.

2. When you get a negative thought in your head, intentionally formulate three positive thoughts.

3. When your thought is a complaint, intentionally formulate a solution, *even if you don't intend to use it.*

4. When dealing with manipulative, negative, or harmful thoughts, ask yourself: *What outcome do I want to see?*

5. Make a list of activities you can do when you are overthinking. Pull these out as needed. After all, doers are not as plagued by bad thoughts. In fact, dwelling on negative thoughts can harm your physical body as well as your mental health.

6. Occupy yourself with something constructive. Although we want to assess our thought life routinely, we should not take up residence in our mind. God did not design

us to live in our heads. This often leads to depression and anxiety. Call someone. Read the Bible or a story out loud. It is harder for negative thoughts to permeate your soul when you are actively engaged in conversation or reading aloud. Go workout. Our bodies are meant to move and be in relationship!

7. Renew your mind. Paul said this:

> Don't copy the behavior and customs of this world, but let God transform you into a new person by changing the way you think. Then you will learn to know God's will for you, which is good and pleasing and perfect. (Romans 12:2)

Keep your mind renewed in the things that you want in your mind and heart. Fellowship with positive people; attend Bible studies or activities with uplifting people. Listen to sermons or positive speakers when you are working out. Be intentional in what you put in your mind because the seeds you plant in your heart will grow provided you continue to give them power through meditation, worry, or rumination. Jesus knew this and taught on this very thing in His Sermon on the Mount.

In the Sermon on the Mount, Jesus shared these thoughts:

> You have heard that our ancestors were told, "You must not murder. If you commit murder, you are subject to judgment." But I say, if you are even angry with someone, you are subject to judgment! (Matthew 5:21–22a)

You have heard the commandment that says, "You must not commit adultery." But I say, anyone who even looks at a woman with lust has already committed adultery with her in his heart. (Matthew 5:27–28)

Now let's see how this plays out. Marty was in his thirties, married, and ran a successful business. He had three children under the age of eleven, and was coming to counseling due to marital struggles and issues with anger. Marty felt that his wife didn't care about him and was only interested in herself. He often talked about her with animosity and unforgiveness. He blamed her that he had to go to counseling and felt that it was her fault that he and his children had a strained relationship. Marty shared that his children did not want to spend time with him. He stated they felt he was angry and miserable. In most of our sessions, Marty had to be redirected to share anything positive or focus energy on change or problem solving. We discussed him attending therapy *with* Susan, his wife, but he was not interested in this option at the time.

Marty was angry because he felt powerless and jealous. He viewed his wife as a happy overcomer who was loved by many. He resented her for not helping him find that favor with those around him. He felt that she should have helped him be happy too. He also held her responsible for repairing the relationship with his children. The resentment and anger he felt toward Susan got deep into his heart. He could not move past it. Yes, he had a mental health diagnosis, but right now I want to focus on his thoughts and how destructive his angry thoughts were.

After several weeks, Marty shared that he had attended a conference and met a very attractive woman. At this juncture, he only regarded her as "attractive." Marty could have held his mind captive to the obedience of Christ when he met this woman. He had a choice as to what to do with his thought. He could have said, "It was very nice to meet you. Excuse me," and walked away to meet with someone else. The only power the thought had over him was what he gave it. In other words, he could exercise responsibility over it; he could receive it or disregard it.

Unfortunately, he wanted the attention of this woman, so he stayed and conversed. They talked the evening away, and when the conference ended and he went home, he was still thinking about Amy. He daydreamed and fantasized about her. He shared that his wife sensed he was not present in their home or relationship. At some point, he friended Amy on social media, and they exchanged numbers. Next thing you knew, they were talking or texting daily. If Marty had held his mind captive to the obedience of Christ, he could have called a friend at his church for support, read his Bible, prayed with his wife, or any number of interventions.

Holding thoughts captive is not a passive process.

Holding thoughts captive is not a passive process. It is something you do, not something you think. When Paul said he would hold the thoughts of the Corinthians captive, he was talking about sharing about Christ and refreshing their minds through discipleship and edification. He was going to refute the claims of the false apostles and back it up with true teaching centered in Christ. We can all do this when our thoughts lead us away from Jesus. The problem with tempting thoughts is that the longer we entertain them, the more they get into our heart. Too often they are easy to entertain. When we don't hold our minds captive to the obedience of Christ, those thoughts permeate our hearts. This is why Jesus said that if you lust after someone in your heart, it is the same as committing adultery.

Week after week, Marty came to counseling and all he wanted to discuss was his relationship with Amy. They grew closer and closer, and each month I saw him deteriorate, as it became increasingly harder to live both lives. His head and heart were at war. From the moment his thoughts turned to Amy, his heart beliefs were supported and created too, and his conflict grew. His intellect told him that ending his marriage was a bad idea. He was hurting his children. He really wasn't giving his marriage a chance. He was not working on the issues that frustrated him. What he was doing was wrong. By now, his heart was telling him that he couldn't fix his marriage. He failed at everything he tried to fix. He had not been able to fix his parent's marriage and his father had left. He believed that he deserved to be happy, but there was no way he could see to be happy in his marriage to Susan. He thought: *Susan doesn't know me or love me like Amy does. Susan and the kids would be okay. I managed when my parents broke up. They will too. I need to do the best thing for my own mental health and needs. Amy is the right choice.*

When your head and heart are in conflict, the heart typically wins. Another way to look at this is that the mind usually loses to the core beliefs the heart has adopted. Almost a year after his introduction to Amy, Marty came in with his wife Susan. Susan had read some of the texts Marty and Amy were sharing. She was devastated. Because the intimate thoughts Marty had toward Amy were deeply planted in Marty's heart, the impact on his marriage and family was destructive. Susan shared that she went through Marty's phone in the first place because of the changes she saw in his relationship with her and their children. Eleven weeks after his introduction to Amy, Marty's heart was no longer held captive to his wife. He no longer wanted to work on the issues in their marriage. He wanted a divorce.

Marty and Susan did get divorced, but his thoughts were causing damage well before Marty ever met Amy. He had been so negative about his marriage for so long, and had ruminated about his unsupportive marriage that he had sown seeds of bitterness in his own heart. Susan

We are designed to be aligned!

had looked at Marty's phone when she noticed changes. He had been distant and preoccupied for months. She admitted that she suspected he was talking to another woman within a month of the conference. When she confronted him or sought reassurance, he just got angry which left her feeling guilty for bringing it up. By the time Susan found evidence, Marty was relieved. He got more and more mentally drained as the conflict within him worsened. He was experiencing memory loss and getting sick frequently, which surprised him as he didn't get sick very often. We are designed to be aligned!

Being in charge of our own thought processes is vitally important to our overall mental health.

> Any form of negative rumination—for example, worrying about your financial future or health—will stimulate the release of destructive neurochemicals. And if you are prone to constantly thinking about negative possibilities and persistently ruminating about problems that have occurred in the past, you may ultimately test positive for clinical depression.[43]

It is important to routinely assess the thoughts we are thinking. Assessing our thought life does not mean we are spending hours or days analyzing them. It means making sure that our anxieties and negative thoughts are not receiving power to support or create heart beliefs that are not based on truth. Heart or core beliefs are difficult to extinguish. There are many examples of lies we frequently believe about ourselves. We might consider ourselves unworthy, unlovable, or incapable. Even when our minds have evidence of the truth, these core beliefs often prevail.

Whenever possible, we need to choose the thoughts on which we meditate and give power. We need to be proactive in using tools to keep our thought life healthy. This does not mean that negative emotions are bad, nor does it mean that we

---

43 Andrew B. Newberg and Mark Robert Waldman, *Words Can Change Your Brain: 12 Conversation Strategies to Build Trust, Resolve Conflict, and Increase Intimacy*, Kindle (New York: A Plume Book, 2013).

need to deny ourselves grief or trauma responses because of their inherent negativity. It means that we need to be grateful and optimistic and meditate on that which is good and godly, even as we deal with negative emotions.

PRINCIPLE 17:
THE WORDS WE SPEAK

> The tongue can bring death or
> life; those who love to talk will
> reap the consequences.
> (Proverbs 18:21)

"Sticks and stones may break my bones but words will never hurt me." Many of us have heard this adage. When I was in school, this was a common response to verbal bullying, but is it true? Can words hurt us?

Definitely! I do appreciate the saying, as it gives power to the person being bullied which may have empowered them from living with a victim identity. Words have great power. Words can condition, build up, and tear down. They can destroy or breathe new life in someone.

As a counselor, words are very important to me. It is my opinion that words are the most powerful tool we possess. In our morning prayer time at Victory

Lives can be changed by the words we speak.

Transformation, I pray that our words will edify, exhort, and encourage. Lives can be changed by the words we speak. Our words can prophesy and help create leaders and teachers. Our words can also discourage, create fear, and disempower people.

Take my youngest son, Dyllon, for example. Dyllon was very smart and had the ability to influence people easily. Once when he was thirteen I received a call from the school district's Food Service Director. It went something like this:

"Hi! Is this Dyllon's mom?"

"Yes," I said, curious as to why I was getting a call.

"I don't know how to tell you this, but you know the $25.00 check you wrote to put in an account for Dyllon?" (She was stammering a bit now.)

"Yes?"

She went on to tell me that Dyllon had somehow managed to get the lady who checked him out in the lunch line to take the check for his lunch. Instead of putting the balance in his account, she cashed the check and gave him the cash. Then he used it to buy gifts from the little school store, and gave them to various girls in his class. Another great dinnertime conversation! I could write another book just on the memories we laugh about at dinner.

Dyllon was good with his words. The problem was that he had ADHD (a family inheritance) and struggled with impulse control and organization among other things. This bright boy with great gifts was struggling in school and extremely unmotivated. He had some teachers that did not even think he was capable. I had met with various teachers over the years to discuss how best to help Dyllon.

When Dyllon was in ninth grade, everything changed. I was finishing up my master's program in social work and took a class on testing and evaluation. Dyllon had a comprehensive psychoeducational evaluation administered by a team of graduate students and a professor from this class. The testing was very revealing about his aptitude and abilities. When we went over the results with the evaluators, Dyllon found out he was intelligent. It blew his mind. In the car on the way home, he kept declaring how smart he was—almost in disbelief. It broke my heart. I listened as Dyllon poured out how so many people in positions of authority in his life had led him to believe that he was stupid, even an idiot. He had heard these words so often that over time he believed them. Being stupid was part of his core belief. I had not told him that he was intelligent and gifted often enough to combat the negative words spoken to him by others.

Additionally, anytime I got frustrated with him, I'd say things like, "Dyllon, this was so easy! Why didn't you get this work done?" This fed that core belief and carried more weight than any time I complimented him on his giftings, probably because he did not receive encouragement in this area from anyone other than me. (Discounting Mom is easy in such a situation.) Even now as an adult in his mid-twenties, those words have power over him and that core belief still permeates. I was telling his girlfriend recently at dinner how brilliant and talented Dyllon was. He rolled his eyes, and said, "Mom, stop." I regret not recognizing that, and wish I had been a more powerful force to help break through those core beliefs he was forming.

This principle has centered on our thoughts. We've explored how we give our thoughts power and how they sow seeds in our hearts. Jesus states in Matthew 12:34 that "out of the abundance of the heart the mouth speaks."

Have you ever engaged in a heated argument only to later regret the words that came out of your mouth? Have you ever apologized, saying you did not mean what you said before? If you have (and we all have), you weren't being truthful. Our mouths do speak what is in our hearts. Your apology should be more like: "I am sorry. I did not mean to say that. I was angry." The distinction here is that you recognize that you did mean what you said, but you didn't mean to say it out loud. Anger often makes us want to hurt someone else. We often think hurtful things in our hearts that we normally do not share or act upon. This apology (and these thoughts) should be followed by prayer in which we ask God to remove these intentions, and help us with our angry thoughts and feelings.

Words spoken in anger are destructive. You can always apologize but once the words are spoken, they are sown and can't be unsaid—or unheard. Romans 12:17 says that faith comes by hearing. In context, Paul is talking about salvation. He's saying we can have faith in Christ after hearing the gospel. However, this idea can be applied to other things too. You can have faith in the wrong thing. It is easy to see that if someone has faith in a person, that person's angry words directed at them can cause a significant level of destruction in their life.

Like Dyllon, I was diagnosed with hyperactivity disorder at the age of eleven. (This is what Attention Deficit Hyperactivity Disorder was called when I was young. This diagnosis is just that: a diagnosis that helped me find solutions and adaptations.

It is not my identity. I truly appreciate the mind that God created for me.)

Aside from having to develop structure and high levels of organization in my life, talking helps me process information. I know what you're thinking: *Her poor husband!* He would agree with you. He is the much quieter one. As we read before, Jesus said we will be judged for every "idle word" (Matt. 12:36). The word *idle* is rendered "careless" or "empty" in some versions. I think I am going to be at that judgment a very long time.

I read the Bible and most books out loud. Doing this helps me with retention and focus. I pray out loud. I also process through things out loud and encourage myself out loud, so if you are wondering if I talk to myself, the answer is yes! Our words are powerful. I was actually talking to myself on a regular basis long before I understood that science had a word for this use of words. It is called selective attention.

Selective attention is defined as "the ability to select and preferentially process specific information while simultaneously suppressing the processing of irrelevant, competing distractors."[44] Speaking or reading out loud helps us focus better and prevents us from being distracted by other things in our environment. Actually verbalizing self-talk out loud as opposed to just thinking those encouraging thoughts has a greater impact

---

44 Elif Isbell et al., "Neuroplasticity of Selective Attention: Research Foundations and Preliminary Evidence for a Gene by Intervention Interaction," *Proceedings of the National Academy of Sciences* 114, no. 35 (2017): pp. 9247–9254, https://doi.org/10.1073/pnas.1707241114.

on goal-directedness by increasing focus and retention while making distractions have less power.[45]

To sum this up, Jesus told us that we will have to give account for what we say and that out of the mouth, the heart speaks. He is telling us to be thoughtful with our words because they represent what is in our hearts—even the careless ones.

> Don't use foul or abusive language. Let everything you say be good and helpful, so that your words will be an encouragement to those who hear them. (Ephesians 4:29)

> Don't speak evil against each other, dear brothers and sisters. If you criticize and judge each other, then you are criticizing and judging God's law. But your job is to obey the law, not to judge whether it applies to you. God alone, who gave the law, is the Judge. He alone has the power to save or to destroy. So what right do you have to judge your neighbor? (James 4:11–12)

Back to sticks and stones. The truth is that is hurting people hurt people. Bullies are not happy people. People that say hurtful things are not happy people—in some aspect of their lives. I have never met anyone who truly wanted to be miserable,

---

45 Nilli Lavie, "Distracted and Confused?: Selective Attention under Load," *Trends in Cognitive Sciences* 9, no. 2 (2005): pp. 75–82, https://doi.org/10.1016/j.tics.2004.12.004.

so why are there so many negative and hurtful words being thrown around? Imagine that every insult, offense, and hurtful word is a seed being planted in the dark garden of someone's mind. Imagine for a moment that your words can cause someone great pain. Many people who were bullied will tell you that the teasing and words being **Hurting people hurt people.** slung at them hurt more than an actual blow. Why? Because the physical wounds healed, while the words planted in the dark garden grew.

Gossip and Slander

> A troublemaker plants seeds of strife; gossip separates the best of friends. (Proverbs 16:28)

I try very hard to pray before, during, and after counseling. I genuinely feel that it is a privilege that people share their lives with me. With that said, I spend a lot of my time listening to people talk about other people. I work hard to help and support positive growth and change in their lives, but even in the most professional of circumstances, it is hard not to gossip. I hear a lot of things about a lot of people. The Scripture that I meditate on, which helps me in counseling the most, is Ephesians 4:29. We've looked at it before, but let's read it in two different versions this time.

> Let no corrupt word proceed out of your mouth, but what is good for necessary edification, that it

may impart grace to the hearers. (Ephesians 4:29 NKJV)

Do not let any unwholesome talk come out of your mouths, but only what is helpful for building others up according to their needs, that it may benefit those who listen. (Ephesians 4:29 NIV)

Many definitions of gossip regard it as rumor spreading. For our purposes, we will use the definition provided by Timothy Hallet, associate professor of the Indiana University sociology department. He defines gossip as "the unsanctioned evaluative talk about people who aren't present." I would also add the term *unconstrained.* When we are discussing gossip at Victory I share that gossip is talking about people when they are not there. People often ask as if to test me, "What if I am saying something nice about someone?" To which I reply, "Good for you." If we all spent all our time saying nice things about people, there would be a lot less depression, social anxiety, and drama in our world.

A study entitled, "Who Gossips and How in Everyday Life?" published in *Social Psychological and Personality Science,* gives us some great insight into gossip. This and other studies suggest that gossip is ubiquitous and helps us establish social norms and share social information.[46] In other words, setting a New Year resolution to stop all forms of gossip would be

---

46 Megan L. Robbins and Alexander Karan, "Who Gossips and How in Everyday Life?," *Social Psychological and Personality Science* 11, no. 2 (February 2019): pp. 185–195, https://doi.org/10.1177/1948550619837000.

futile. Gossip is helpful. According to the study, most gossip is either neutral or positive and discusses people with whom we are acquainted. About 11% of gossip is negative with most negative gossip being shared by young adults. However, gossip is evaluative and can be helpful in interpreting your world.[47] An example would be when Monique shared with her friends that Phil had cheated on her multiple times in the past four months and the couple broke up. Is this negative gossip? Yes. Assuming that what Monique shared was true, is it malicious? It doesn't appear to be from this brief description. Is it useful? It could be since Monique was talking to a group of close friends. Monique shared information about someone's behavior for others to evaluate. We can also assume that Monique was seeking support from her friends after a painful relationship. We can quickly change the status of this gossip in an instant by adding the words, "I heard…." For example, if Monique was talking to her friends and said, "I heard that Leslie's boyfriend has cheated on her several times in the last four months," this is a rumor. A rumor is "a current story passing from one person to another, without any known authority for its truth."[48]

In our example, Monique is passing on third party information. Let's reread Ephesians 4:29: "Let everything you say be good and helpful, so that your words will be an encouragement to those who hear them."

---

47 Ibid.

48 "Rumor Definition & Meaning," *Webster's Unabridged Dictionary*, part of the public domain at Project Gutenberg.

It may appear that I am promoting speaking negatively about people. I am not. I am illustrating a difference in sharing. Intention is the important thing to think about here.

It wasn't my Christian principles that led me to be thoughtful about gossip. It was watching the destruction it caused. I often pray for my counselees and ask others to do so. There are people in my community that lift my counseling in prayer regularly. This moved me greatly and never occurred to me that anyone would think to do that, but I need that covering.

People share everything from how their spouse hurt their feelings to horrifying incidences of child abuse and other personal violations. About seven years ago, I felt the need to ask for forgiveness because I was harboring unforgiveness towards people I wasn't even counseling—some I hadn't even met. I need to regularly and repeatedly forgive the people that my counselees talk about. I love my work passionately and I love being available so that people have someone safe to talk to. This is a real part of my job and I received a lot of training to deal with such situations.

Recently I realized that the unforgiveness I had towards people by association through counseling results in the same thing that happens when people gossip. It made me realize the importance of two things: praying for the people that my patients were sharing about and teaching those I counsel to pray for the people who hurt them.

Before I was saved, I fully and intentionally participated in gossip. Gossip is unconstrained conversation and reports about other people. It is always a quick and easy way to feel good about yourself. After all, you are guaranteeing that someone will be interested in what you have to say about someone else. It grants one a false sense of empowerment when they can discuss intimate details about someone else behind their back. People long to hear the information and that makes you feel very important. But by definition, gossip isn't bad; it's just the hurtful, slanderous, and sometimes malicious remarks and conversation that are extremely harmful.

You can gossip about people and say positive things, but it is often a tantalizing temptation to regurgitate rumors instead. You are the repeater, not the source. This is strongly evidenced in social media and through email chains. Take the Obama Phone for example. The Lifeline program was developed in the Reagan era and offered low cost phone service to low-income families. In 2008, Safelink Wireless offered the first free government cell phone because by this time, people were more likely to have cell phones instead of landlines. Obama was elected in November of 2008, and the first Safelink phones were distributed during the Bush administration. Since 2009 (and resurfacing periodically), I began getting emails disparaging Obama for giving free phones to the poor, mostly from friends and family. The issue with the email was that it was perpetuating false information to defame another. I am not trying to make a political statement. I am just trying to say that we often use gossip to support and validate our beliefs without any concern for the truth.

On another occasion, I politely replied to a friend's email that had been sent to a large group, pointing out that the email was making false claims. I shared the evidence showing the mistake and he got angry with me! I had expected him to say

"Thank you so much for clarifying that" or something to that effect, but that never happened because the lie supported his beliefs, so he just kept sharing it.

Every Monday our advocacy team at Victory gets together to go over our weekly case reviews. We are all sitting around talking about people. As we do, we are constantly reminded that our hearts need to be focused on the healing and betterment of the people with whom we are working.

When I catch myself gossiping, I stop and repent. I really do hate gossip. It can be so evil and destructive. It is easy to get enticed into gossiping—particularly if you are surrounded by those that simply can't contain their need to talk about other people when they are not present.

The Bible says this: "Rumors are dainty morsels that sink deep into one's heart" (Prov. 18:8). Sometimes people participate carefully by using *qualifiers*. We qualify when we say things like: "John is really rude. I can't believe he treats her that way, *but* [qualifier] maybe he is just having a hard time with being alone so much since she got promoted and is now traveling for work.." I have even listened to gossip in prayer circles! Sometimes we just listen, but we are still a participant when we do that. Don't kid yourself.

I was formerly the executive director of a mental health organization that had a drop-in center. I strictly prohibited gossip. If gossip can destroy typical people, imagine what it does to people with severe and persistent mental illness. Staff knew that they could be fired if caught gossiping or encouraging it in our day programs or activities. The "no gossip policy" occurred because of a situation in which participants were talking about a young, single mom who struggled with bipolar disorder. The gossip focused on her parenting and a recent relationship she was in. It became so severe and vicious that the victim ended up at the local inpatient mental health unit for two weeks, completely broken down.

As a result of this experience, Victory Transformation has the same no gossip policy.

Gossip is defined as casual or unconstrained conversation or reports about other people, typically involving details that are not confirmed as being true. Note that it doesn't indicate that only negative words constitute gossip.

Lisa had some counseling last year. She was struggling in her seventeen-year marriage. She loved her husband, but he was controlling and verbally abusive, and this had gone on for many years. She didn't want to leave him; she wanted healthy supports and strategies to cope with it. One of the things she shared with me was how supportive her friends were. She had over 700 of them on social media, and routinely posted her needs for prayer or support.

She was always careful to omit precisely what she needed prayer for, and friends would private message her with any questions. Soon she had a large group of friends to talk to every time she posted anything about the difficulties she was having at home.

Prior to her coming to see me, things came to a head with her husband. He was on her social media too. He was ready to leave. She had reached out for support to her friends to help keep her marriage together, but they were encouraging her to leave. After all, she had spent the last few years lamenting about how awful and abusive her husband was. She actually lost friends when she told them she wanted to make her marriage work.

His words disparaged her and her words were gossip about him. Lisa was getting a fix. Every time Glen tore her down with his words, she sought "feel good" support and encouragement through social media. The more negative information she shared, the more support and encouragement she received. The encouragement helped her get through her days during those difficult times. However, once she resolved to stay with him and make things work, she had to struggle with the judgment and criticism she received from those same friends.

She came into counseling the following week very upset. When asked what was wrong, Lisa stated, "I am really trying to make things work and Glen is trying too. He is even looking at getting his own counselor." Then she sighed. "The problem is my friends hate me now. They think I am an idiot to stay in this situation. Some of them unfriended me and others won't talk to me at all."

Gossip can be destructive and divisive. Many of the people with whom Lisa was sharing her plight were not friends outside of the social network. We identified about sixty of them as friends, but most of these were people she had relationships with through her church and the community. (Yes, we loosely went through her friends list.) She had thirty separate messenger threads complaining about her husband. She did not know twenty of these were people outside social media. Many were friends of her friends.

Eventually an elder in her church came to the couple about their marital problems. Although they were not interested in meeting regularly with the elder, it was apparent that their marriage problems in their marriage were no longer a private matter.

Here are some practical suggestions to help combat slanderous gossip and develop positive, encouraging relationships.

- If I am part of a conversation in which someone begins talking about someone not present *and* there is no positive outcome for the conversation (i.e., let's plan Larry's surprise birthday party), then I suggest we stop having the conversation.

- In counseling, whenever possible, I try reframing all situations so that we are speaking about the solution, *not* the problem. When your words are constantly stating negative things, your behavior will align. (I understand that people may need to work through things and process them, but it is much easier when one can see the light at the end of the tunnel.)

- If you have a problem with someone, seek to involve them in the solution. This is the directive Jesus gave in Matthew 18:15 (NLT): "If another believer sins against you, go privately and point out the offense. If the other person listens and confesses it, you have won that person back." Venting is not a biblical directive. Instead of talking about the person, go to the person. Jesus said if we can resolve the issue with them, we gain that person back.

- If someone is sincerely seeking counsel on a matter, be responsible when discussing people. If you feel a sense of guilt in the conversation, your conscience might be telling you something. Words hurt. Please be careful.
- Be proactive; and wherever possible, don't allow bad thoughts time to form in the first place. This may mean removing yourself from potentially toxic situations or removing toxic things from your life.
- My husband and I have a great relationship, but when we used to argue, both of us were very hurtful with our words. (Remember, hurting people hurt people.) Bill would send me text after text filled with angry words. I learned quickly to delete them without looking. Once the words in the texts were in my mind, it was easy for them to sink into my heart. In addition to hearing them (reading is an auditory process) we "say" the words in our head. Once we see them, we can't "unsee" them. Bill and I would bury the hatchet, but I didn't want to start harboring unforgiveness or resentment toward him as a result of reading his texts. Those messages are no longer part of our marriage but had I read them, I don't know how they would have impacted me. Definitely not positively! I often advise others not to read angry or manipulative texts. Just delete them. If someone needs to know what is in a text message because of children, but there is a history of venomous messages that tear the reader down, have someone else that is safe read the text. If there is no useful information in it, have that person delete it.

Ephesians 4:29 instructs us to use words that are edifying, good, and helpful. We can change the world with our words. Imagine what it would be like if everyone sought to intentionally speak words which build people up. This doesn't mean you never speak negative words. Correction builds people up. It means that before we speak, we should always be thoughtful.

Case in point. I found myself often speaking defensively in certain situations. Someone in gentle correction shared with me that this was pride and explained why

> **We can change the world with our words.**

defensiveness was rooted in pride. He helped me understand that it was a desire to justify behavior. I didn't see it as pride because I wasn't being haughty. I just often felt that I had to defend my decisions and actions. The sin of pride is being overly preoccupied with yourself or with your status, achievements, or possessions. Often this comes from insecurity, but it is still an excessive preoccupation with self. Always feeling the need to defend myself was rooted in insecurity, but that didn't change the fact that my defensiveness was prideful. I began working on this behavior and was grateful for the honesty of a friend.

Here are some helpful tips:

- When you find yourself complaining or speaking negatively, intentionally speak positive words and solutions.
- Make a list of people that you intentionally wish to encourage and speak positive words over them daily. The list is not meant to help you contrive positive words, it is meant to keep this practice in the forefront of your mind.

If you are thinking positive thoughts about someone, take the time to let them know, even if it is just a quick text.

- Be brief with your words. Research shows that short sentences are less likely to evoke or perpetuate anger and other negative emotions.[49]

- Speak slowly. (This takes much practice for me.) When we speak slowly, we reduce stress for both the speaker and the listener and foster greater understanding of what is being said.[50]

- Practice selective attention. Read out loud and practice self-talk aloud. This can help you retain information better and be less distracted.[51]

- Avoid slander, unwholesome talk, and rumors. "Keep your tongue from speaking evil and your lips from telling lies!" (Psa. 34:13). If you have an issue with someone, go to the person and bring up your concern as directed in Matthew 18:15, but don't share it with someone else.

- Be thoughtful about how you engage in conversation that is stressful or while you are stressed. Although it may be unavoidable, be mindful of your words. According to authors Dr. Andrew Newberg and Mark Robert Waldman, stress causes interference with the neurology related to

---

49 Andrew B. Newberg and Mark Robert Waldman, *Words Can Change Your Brain: 12 Conversation Strategies to Build Trust, Resolve Conflict, and Increase Intimacy*, Kindle (New York: A Plume Book, 2013).

50 Ibid.

51 Nilli Lavie, "Distracted and Confused?: Selective Attention under Load," *Trends in Cognitive Sciences* 9, no. 2 (2005): pp. 75–82, https://doi.org/10.1016/j.tics.2004.12.004.

"language production and perception." When we are stressed, "the emotional circuits of the limbic brain become active, and the language circuits in the frontal lobe become less active."[52]

Jesus talked about building people up with our words. He talked about love, peace, and joy—the greatest blessings from heaven. However, we have to choose them. Paul encouraged us to meditate on what is good:

> Finally, brethren, whatever things are true, whatever things are noble, whatever things are just, whatever things are pure, whatever things are lovely, whatever things are of good report, if there is any virtue and if there is anything praiseworthy—meditate on these things. The things which you learned and received and heard and saw in me, these do, and the God of peace will be with you.
> (Philippians 4:8–9 NKJV)

Authors Dr. Andrew Newberg and Mark Robert Waldman state that "a single word has the power to influence the expression of genes that regulate physical and emotional stress."[53]

When we use positive words instead of negative words we increase our motivation, spurring ourselves into action,

---

52 Andrew B. Newberg and Mark Robert Waldman, *Words Can Change Your Brain: 12 Conversation Strategies to Build Trust, Resolve Conflict, and Increase Intimacy*, Kindle (New York: A Plume Book, 2013).

53 Ibid.

and changing the way we see things. When we speak positive words to others, we truly are *blessing them*.

Scripture shows us that spoken blessings were taken seriously. They were not empty salutations. Jesus knew the power of our words. In Luke 10:5, He sent the disciples out and told them, "Whenever you enter someone's home, first say, 'May God's peace be on this house'" (NLT).

It is important that we take our words seriously. The words we speak about ourselves and others can form core beliefs and wounds that are hard to heal. Our words can also help build people up and help them achieve great things. This principle is inherent in, and can be applied to, every other principle in this book. Use your words to encourage people. Use your words to pray for and bless people. Use your words to edify the people around you.

I hope you found this collection of experiences and observations useful. I pray that God blesses you and reveals to you all that can heal, give hope, and create peace and joy in your life. Thank you so much for the privilege of sharing my life with you as so many people have shared their lives with me.

ABOUT THE AUTHOR

Daun Whittaker is the founder and retired executive director of Victory Transformation, Inc., a local mission in Oswego, New York, that helps people who are homeless or have critical needs get on their feet again through love, life skills, counseling, and support.

Daun has dedicated her life to working with people in poverty and other vulnerable populations, such as those with disabilities, mental health issues, and victims of domestic violence.

Since 2009, Daun has been counseling in her private practice. She received her master's in social work from Syracuse University and is a licensed clinical social worker. She is also a certified psychiatric rehabilitation practitioner and holds a doctorate of theology in Christian counseling from Summit Bible College in Bakersfield, California.

Visit Daun at her website: www.DaunW.com

IF YOU ENJOYED THIS BOOK, WILL YOU HELP ME SPREAD THE WORD?

There are several ways you can help me get the word out about the message of this book...

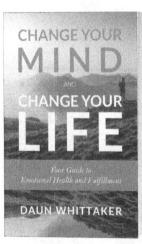

- Post a 5-Star review on Amazon.
- Write about the book on your Facebook, Twitter, Instagram, LinkedIn, – any social media you regularly use!
- If you blog, consider referencing the book, or publishing an excerpt from the book with a link back to my website. You have my permission to do this if you provide proper credit and backlinks.
- Recommend the book to friends – word-of-mouth is still the most effective form of advertising.
- Purchase additional copies to give away as gifts on my website at www.daunw.com.

The best way to connect is by visiting: www.daunw.com

Printed in the USA
CPSIA information can be obtained
at www.ICGtesting.com
JSHW011941171023
50214JS00006B/4